Lea M. McGee

Transforming
Literacy Practices
in Preschool

Research-Based Practices
That Give All Children
the Opportunity to Reach
Their Potential as Learners

NEW YORK • TORONTO • LONDON • AUCKLAND • SYDNEY
MEXICO CITY • NEW DELHI • HONG KONG • BUENOS AIRES

Dedication

I dedicate this book to every preschool child and teacher
who has taught me what I needed to know.

Scholastic grants teachers permission to photocopy the reproducible pages from this book for classroom use. No other part
of this publication may be reproduced in whole or in part, or stored in a retrieval system, or transmitted in any form or by
any means, electronic, mechanical, photocopying, recording, or otherwise, without permission of the publisher. For
information regarding permission, write to Scholastic Inc., 557 Broadway, New York, NY 10012.

Cover design by Maria Lilja
Interior design by Sarah Morrow
Acquiring Editor: Margery Rosnick
Editor: Joan Irwin
Production Editor: Carol Ghiglieri
Copy Editor: Chris Borris

1 2 3 4 5 6 7 8 9 10   40   13 12 11 10 09 08 07

Contents

Foreword

by Lesley Mandel Morrow
Rutgers the State University of New Jersey

In the past ten years, it has become more and more apparent that universal preschool is a necessity. Children who have a limited vocabulary at the age of 3 because of limited experiences are already "at risk" for success in school. However, research has demonstrated that if these children go to a quality preschool that has a strong language and literacy program, they can catch up to their peers. Research studies have demonstrated that children who go to quality preschools are more likely to learn to read, do well in elementary school, graduate from high school, exhibit socially acceptable behavior as older children and adults, earn more than those who are not literate, and have children who learn to read as well.

Lea McGee's *Transforming Literacy Practices in Preschool* makes an important contribution to early childhood education by clearly demonstrating best practice for preschool instruction. This book has it all: it's well-written, reader-friendly, research-based, and most of all, timely. Lea lets us know that we must teach preschool children using direct instructional strategies, and she provides a range of appropriate strategies and activities for young children. Her writing style is inviting, and the chapters clearly outline what needs to be taught. Throughout the book, you'll encounter excerpts that include dialogue from the classroom to demonstrate a strategy or idea, making the book truly come alive. And

I particularly like the appendix, which provides monthly goals for 3-year-olds and 4-year-olds. I have not seen this type of presentation before and know it will be of tremendous value to teachers.

With her Early Reading First grant, Lea spent an enormous amount of time in a variety of preschool classrooms, helping with professional development and studying what works best. This book includes the wealth of knowledge she gained from her rich experiences in these rooms. *Transforming Literacy Practices in Preschool* should be required reading for all preschool teachers. It will help them to understand how we need to think about preschool children, the environment in which they learn, and how we can teach them so they become literate and successful older children and adults.

Introduction

Over the past few years I have been working as a director of and consultant for several Early Reading First grants. These experiences provided me with opportunities to learn about ways in which educators working together can transform language and literacy programs for young children. Through these projects, I gained new insights into the practical applications of research in the classroom and the ways in which innovative teachers make literacy come alive for young children. All of us involved in these projects acknowledged the value of experience; however, we also understood that programs and instructional practices must have a research base in order to be credible. Because my role was to provide leadership and guidance in what would need to be done in order to meet the requirements of the Early Reading First grant, I delved deeply into the research in preschool literacy. I worked closely with early childhood educators to examine existing practices and to explore ways to implement research-based practices that would transform the preschool literacy program.

When teachers improve the quality of their language and literacy environment and the quality of their curriculum, children's language and literacy concepts accelerate (Dickinson & Sprague, 2001).

This book describes instructional practices in literacy that several teachers implemented as we worked together on the Early Reading First projects. The purpose of Early Reading First is to ensure that preschool children enter kindergarten prepared to succeed in a variety of literacy tasks. We were focused on crafting and implementing a vision of "Transformed Literacy and Language Best Practices" that included revisiting standards, examining the classroom environment, and expanding our practice to include both embedded, child-centered activities and direct, systematic instruction. Throughout the book, you will find examples of how individual teachers used various research-based instructional strategies. Each of us has something to tell about the practices that transform preschool literacy instruction and what happens when we use strategies that foster children's language growth and development. Developing an environment of collegiality and open communication is an important feature of any effort designed to support teachers in modifying their instructional practices. The success of the Early Reading First projects in which I was involved derived from the collaborative participation of the preschool educators who were involved in the projects. I hope their voices are evident as you read this book.

Preschool programs have been available for many years. Traditionally, these programs have focused on providing nurturing custodial care and promoting social interactions among children and other adults outside the immediate family. More recently, the purpose has expanded to include a greater focus on cognitive and language development within nurturing and stimulating environments. Today, preschool teachers are expected to provide instructional activities that prepare children for more formal literacy instruction in kindergarten and the primary school years. This emphasis on preschool language and literacy development provides new opportunities for teachers to modify their practice in ways that are emotionally engaging and intellectually challenging for children. Transformed literacy practices provide experiences that can contribute to life-changing accelerations in children's motivation for achievement and in their overall development. Preschools that provide high-quality language and literacy programs can make a difference for all children. Furthermore, such programs can make a difference in closing the gap low-income children experience even before entering kindergarten.

Classroom Environment

A variety of research has contributed insights into the characteristics of classroom environments that provide optimum support for language and literacy development. The findings from various studies reveal the following:

- Books must be plentiful in the classroom, teachers should regularly read aloud to children, and children should have frequent opportunities to interact with books on their own (Neuman, 1999).

- Children's dramatic-play spaces should be themed and include props that encourage them to pretend to read and write (Morrow & Rand, 1991; Neuman & Roskos, 1993, 1997; Roskos & Neuman, 2001).

- Adults need to be present in these centers, following children's lead in play but providing opportunities for extended conversations. Children should see teachers model writing for a variety of purposes in order to extend children's awareness of different functions of print and to support their pretend writing (Neuman & Roskos, 1992).

What Is Early Reading First?

Early Reading First is a program authorized under Subpart 2, Part B, Title I of the ESEA, as enacted by the No Child Left Behind Act, 2001, Public Law 107-110. The purpose of Early Reading First is to insure that preschool children enter kindergarten prepared to succeed. The stated goal of these programs is to use Early Reading First grants to create Centers of Educational Excellence that will provide high-quality education to preschool children, especially children from low-income families. Organizations that receive Early Reading First grants are required to use scientifically based research to create classroom environments that will be rich in age-appropriate print, including displaying the alphabet where it is visible to children, and providing many books and ample materials to encourage writing. Teachers will deliver "intentional and explicit instruction" (Early Reading First Preliminary Guidance, 2002, p. 4) and use activities that will insure the age-appropriate development of "oral language (vocabulary, expressive language, listening comprehension), phonological awareness (rhyming, blending, segmenting), print awareness, and alphabet knowledge (letter recognition)" (p. 4).

Early Reading First grants are to be used to "transform existing early education programs" into "centers of early learning excellence" (Early Reading First Preliminary Guidance, 2002, p. 5). The guidance provided to potential grantees stressed that the classroom environment, curriculum, instruction, assessment, and professional development as well as children's achievement in existing preschool programs of all types was to be transformed. While not directly stated in the grant, it was clear that the federal government was interested in using Early Reading First funds to find organizations that were willing and able to tackle the arduous task of transforming ordinary classrooms and effective teachers into extraordinary classrooms staffed by highly effective, exemplary teachers.

- Classroom displays should include a variety of print that is valued by and useful to children and teachers (Taylor, Blum, & Logsdon, 1986).

- Classroom schedules should allow frequent opportunities for adults and children to have extended conversations and experiences attempting to read and write.

These physical and child-adult interaction attributes are well documented in research literature and generally accepted as indicators of high-quality language- and print-rich environments.

Instructional Approaches: Embedded and Direct Instruction

Embedded instruction and direct instruction are two approaches commonly used in preschool literacy programs. Proponents of embedded instruction advocate for child-centered instruction, which they consider to be developmentally appropriate (IRA/NAEYC, 1998). In contrast, other early childhood professionals express the need for direct, systematic instruction in skills shown to be foundational for reading and writing (NICHD, 2000). Research supports the effectiveness of both child-centered, embedded instruction and direct, systematic instruction (Justice & Ezell, 2002; Justice et al., 2003).

Embedded instruction occurs as teachers read or write with children to serve a real purpose (for example, they read aloud a book for children to enjoy a funny story or write an enlarged version of a thank you letter to a class visitor). During these activities, embedded within their larger purpose of enjoyment or communicating a thank you, teachers also draw children's attention to print. They might talk about the letters they are writing or might remind children that they are turning to the next page to read. These activities provide children with meaningful experiences from which they learn that reading and writing are valuable tools that will help them in many things in life.

Embedded literacy instruction can take place during dramatic-play, interactive read-aloud, shared reading, and shared-writing activities. With the teacher's guidance, children develop concepts about the functions and purposes of reading and writing that are prerequisites for later learning about the finer details of how print works, such as learning letter names or letter-sound relationships (Lomax & McGee, 1987; Purcell-Gates, 1996). For this reason, instructional activities designed to help children focus on alphabet letters, attend to sounds in spoken words, and match letters to sounds should often use texts that make sense to and serve purposes that are evident to children (such as when they dictate a list of possible activities that they would like to do on an upcoming field trip). Research has documented that children who have acquired many concepts about how print functions more easily and successfully acquire conventional skills associated with beginning reading and writing instruction in first grade (Purcell-Gates & Dahl, 1991). Thus, it is critical that teachers provide children with daily experience reading texts that are meaningful and with writing experiences that are purposeful.

Embedded approaches are more systematic when teachers plan a series of lessons in which they read books aloud for enjoyment, but also plan a few highly crafted interactions each time they read that are focused on directing attention to a single skill or concept. For example, teachers repeatedly ask specific kinds of questions that draw attention to particular alphabet letters as they read aloud Big Books. This is in contrast to pointing out alphabet letters at random or only in response to children's comments and questions. Therefore, carefully planned, purposeful, embedded literacy activities will extend children's awareness of the variety of language forms found in print intended to serve a variety of purposes.

Direct, systematic instruction trains children in the use of a specific skill through sequenced lessons that gradually increase in difficulty (Adams, Foorman, Lundberg, & Beeler, 1998; Snow, Burns, & Griffin, 1998). At the preschool level, this type of instruction is frequently used to help children develop skill in phonemic awareness and phonics. For example, in one program teaching rhyme, teachers read a rhyming book or poem that contains at least ten rhyme pairs and that matches a topic of ongoing class interest (van Kleek, Gillam, & McFadden, 1998). After reading the poem, the teachers made rhyming games and engaged children in a carefully selected set of activities sequenced from easier to more difficult. Training is an important element in direct, systematic instruction, particularly when children are

Continuum of Children's Development in Early Reading and Writing

Phase 1: Awareness and exploration (goals for preschool)

Children explore their environment and build the foundations for learning to read and write.

Children can

- Enjoy listening to and discussing storybooks
- Understand that print carries a message
- Engage in reading and writing attempts
- Identify labels and signs in their environment
- Participate in rhyming games
- Identify some letter and make some letter-sound matches
- Use known letters or approximations of letters to represent written language (especially meaningful words like their name and phrases such as "I love you")

What teachers do

- Share books with children, including Big Books, and model reading behaviors
- Talk about letters by name and sounds
- Establish a literacy-rich environment
- Reread favorite stories
- Engage children in language games
- Promote literacy-related play activities
- Encourage children to experiment with writing

From Learning to Read and Write: Developmentally Appropriate Practices for Young Children*, a joint position statement of the International Reading Association and the National Association for the Education of Young Children. Copyright ©1998.*

Note: This list is intended to be illustrative, not exhaustive. Children at any grade level will function at a variety of phases along the reading/writing continuum.

developing phonological awareness (Snow, Burns, & Griffin, 1998). The word *training* implies that instruction should be focused on the skill at hand directly from, rather than taught embedded in, reading or writing activities.

There is ample research confirming that children do acquire many foundational concepts through instruction that could be considered systematic and direct. Researchers have taught preschool children to identify alphabet letters (Roberts & Neal, 2004), write their names (Justice et al., 2003), and recognize words with the same beginning phonemes (Byrne & Fielding-Barnsley, 1991).

Research, however, suggests that embedded approaches are also effective for helping children learn foundational concepts. For example, when teachers read aloud Big Books and frequently ask questions drawing children's attention to specific alphabet letters, children learn more alphabet letters (Justice & Ezell, 2002). When teachers stop as they read aloud a book with rhyming words to model isolating a few rhyming words into their phonemes and help children count the number of phonemes, children are better able to segment words (Ukrainetz et al., 2000).

The point is this: No one teaching method or approach is likely to be effective for all children. Knowledgeable teachers use a variety of strategies— some that are characteristic of embedded instruction and others that are characteristic of direct instruction. Both types of instruction are described in this book. Chapter 3 examines embedded instruction in reading aloud and dramatizing activities, and Chapter 4 describes embedded instruction in writing. In Chapter 5, direct instruction is described for developing vocabulary, alphabet recognition, concepts about print, and emergent reading. Direct instruction in phonemic awareness, alphabetic principle, and writing through invented spelling is described in Chapter 6. These chapters present examples of best practice, based on both research and theory, that includes both child-centered, embedded and direct, systematic instruction.

Teachers Who Inspired This Book

Now I'd like you to meet five teachers with whom I had the privilege of working in the Early Reading First projects. Their willingness to change their practices and share their insights into children's literacy development enlightened me in ways I had not even considered at the beginning of the projects. You will find examples of their instructional practices and reflective comments throughout the chapters in this book.

Ede Wortham has been a pre-kindergarten teacher at Just 4 Developmental Laboratory in Mobile, Alabama, for 12 years. Ede's school serves low-income children from all over the city of Mobile. All children accepted at the school were screened in the spring before school entry and selected as having the lowest scores on a standardized early childhood readiness test. During the time that I worked with Ede, she had 17 children in her classroom (16 African American and 1 Caucasian), and 13 qualified for free or reduced-cost lunch.

Linda Rodgers has taught at Head Start for 18 years. She had 17 children in her classroom (12 African American and 5 Caucasian) at the time that I worked with her. Linda was adept at integrating Early Reading First project activities into what is required in Head Start programs. She rearranged her room, changed her schedule, adopted the project literacy curriculum, and integrated monthly language and literacy standards with the Head Start framework.

Kay Armstrong teaches 4-year-olds in a state-funded pre-kindergarten classroom in Greenville, Alabama. This is only one of 50 preschools funded by the Office of School Readiness (OSR) in Alabama. OSR stipulates that all children in the community are eligible to enroll and are selected on a first come, first served basis. Enrollment is limited to 18 children. Kay's class had a mixture of children from low-income and middle-income families with about 50 percent of the children qualifying for free or reduced-cost lunch.

Annie Walker and Katesha Washington co-teach 4-year-olds in a day care center in a small town in rural Mississippi. They were part of Project CORE (Community of Reading Excellence), a 2004 Early Reading First grant awarded to the University of Alabama. They were also part of Head Start Cooperative, and taught 16 low-income African American children. Some of the children stay at the day care center all day, from 7:45 a.m. until as late as 6:00 p.m., while other children leave on the Head Start bus in early afternoon. Annie and Katesha work together to deliver whole and small group instruction, center time, snack and other mealtimes, outdoor play, and nap time.

What You Will Find in This Book

My goal in these pages is to provide preschool teachers with information that will assist them in creating their own centers of excellence. I designed this book to help you become more effective in teaching language and literacy in ways that are appropriate and motivating for all children in preschool. I provide research evidence for instructional strategies and show how these strategies function in the reality of the classroom. As a result of the Early Reading First research project on which this book is based, these strategies have successfully met the tests of children's interest and teacher acceptance. Presumably, you will be able to picture yourself and your students in the activities as you read this book. More importantly, I hope that you will actually use the activities with your students.

CHAPTER 1

Transforming the Preschool Literacy Curriculum

A curriculum is the resource that provides the framework for instructional planning. There are a variety of curricula available for preschool programs. One kind encompasses activities in each area of child development, including language and literacy. Most examples of this type of curriculum offer suggested activities and guidelines on the nature of appropriate instruction and give teachers considerable latitude in selecting activities based on observations of children and their needs, interests, and learning styles.

Other curricula focus only on language and literacy development. There is a wide range of these curricula, with more appearing each year as the importance of preschool language and literacy becomes more prominent. These curricula range from highly scripted (lessons are sequenced and teachers are told what to say), to moderately scripted (a variety of lessons for each day are suggested and examples of how to deliver instruction are provided), to mildly scripted (teachers can select units and activities within those units in any order they choose).

Using Monthly Goals for Instruction

Rather than merely adopting a curriculum, I suggest another kind of plan that will enable you to effectively transform your language and literacy program. With this plan, you can identify monthly goals and the kinds of instructional activities that should be provided to help children reach those goals. The goals serve as a guide to select activities from any curriculum. Used in this way, the monthly goals enable you to transform the curriculum to accommodate children's instructional needs. As you observe children's learning during the months in the program, you can make adjustments in the goals and fine-tune your instruction to target areas where children need more direction and practice, or even more challenging activities.

In the appendix, you will find two sets of monthly goals: Monthly Goals for 3-year-olds and Monthly Goals for 4-year-olds. It is important to keep in mind that you can use these monthly goals as guidelines for selecting instructional activities. You can determine whether children are successful in participating in the learning activities and are acquiring concepts specified in the monthly goals. At times, you may need to adjust the goals that you expect children to achieve and modify your instruction accordingly. Small group instructional activities that are intended to help children meet monthly goals should introduce children to new concepts. These activities should provide enough frequent practice with the new concepts that you can be confident that over several days of instruction, children are making progress. If this is not the case, then the goals are too challenging and not achievable, and likely highly frustrating to

Teacher Reflection

Kay Armstrong shared these observations about her experience in using monthly goals. "One of the first things I learned as a part of the Early Reading First project was the set of overall goals for children in phonemic awareness, alphabet recognition, concepts about prints, and vocabulary. I've discovered that children can do so much more than I ever thought. I think over what I want them to learn, and then I search for some activities that I know will appeal to the children.

both you and the children. On the other hand, if children can easily demonstrate mastery, then other more challenging activities need to be presented.

Using Assessments to Monitor Children's Achievement of Monthly Goals

Frequent monitoring of children's achievement provides a critical feedback loop to the content of monthly goals and to selecting instructional activities. At a minimum, you should assess children's ability to write their names and other literacy concepts four times per year. Figure 1.1 shows a literacy monitoring assessment tool that will help you determine children's ability to identify upper- and lowercase alphabet letters, isolate beginning phonemes, and identify beginning letters that correspond to the initial phoneme. It is not necessary to use all these assessments at each monitoring time. For example:

For 3-year-olds, it may be appropriate merely to ask children to write their names and to identify the first letter in their name. Later, 3-year-olds might be asked to write their names and to identify the uppercase letters.

For 4-year-olds, particularly after several months of instruction in both alphabet identification and learning beginning sounds, you could administer the entire monitoring assessment tool.

This tool is easy to use. First, you need to prepare index cards on which each of the upper- and lowercase letters shown in Figure 1.1 are printed. Begin by showing the children the uppercase letters and then ask them to find letters that they know. Children can flip over the cards and name the letters they know. Using the monitoring score sheet in Figure 1.1, put a circle around letters children know and an "x" over letters they don't know. When children know many uppercase letters, you can assess their knowledge of lowercase letters. To assess whether children have learned to identify the beginning phoneme of a word, read aloud the words presented in Figure 1.1 and ask children to "say the beginning sound." Some children will say the letter name rather than the sound. When this occurs, say, "That is the letter name. Tell me the sound." When children know many alphabet letters and can say many beginning sounds of words, you should read aloud the list of words and ask children to "Tell me the letter this word begins with."

This assessment is very quick to administer and provides a quarterly overview of what children are learning in two critical areas of early literacy. This assessment, of course, does not measure all that children should be learning.

Figure 1.1 Example Monitoring Score Sheet

Identifying Uppercase Letters

Circle correct, X incorrect

M	T	S	K	A	O	
W	B	R	N	C	E	Z
X	D	P	Y	F	Q	H
V	G	L	U	J	I	

UPPERCASE TOTAL _____

Identifying Lowercase Letters

Circle correct, X incorrect

m	t	s	k	a	o	
w	b	r	n	c	e	z
x	d	y	f	h	v	g
p	l	u	j	i	q	

LOWERCASE TOTAL _____

Isolating Beginning Phoneme and Identifying Beginning Letter

Circle correct, X incorrect

Isolate beginning phoneme			Identify beginning letter
/b/	1.	bug	B
/g/	2.	goat	G
/h/	3.	hat	H
/j/	4.	jump	J
/t/	5.	toe	T
/m/	6.	man	M
/g/	7.	gum	G
/d/	8.	duck	D
/l/	9.	light	L
/s/	10.	sun	S

BEGINNING PHONEME TOTAL _____   BEGINNING LETTER TOTAL _____

Identifying Children at Risk

It is clear that while most children will meet a program's challenging but achievable goals, some children will not. Many preschools include children who have been identified with developmental delays or language impairments, other children will later be identified as having special needs, still other children will be English Language Learners (ELLs). These categories of children are considered at risk for later having difficulties in learning to read and write. Low-income children are also often identified as having high risk factors. Transforming preschools into Centers of Educational Excellence means that teachers will not automatically consider these children at risk. Rather, based on children's responses to instruction and the results of frequent monitoring of children's learning, teachers may identify children who need more intensive intervention services.

In preschool, at-risk children who might benefit from more intensive intervention services are those who have not made observable progress in meeting monthly goals when they have been provided high-quality and targeted instruction. These children may need instruction that is delivered in very small groups or even one-on-one. The percentage of these children should be very small even in programs serving primarily low-income children. Research has shown that instruction in fairly large groups (although smaller than whole group) can accelerate language and literacy development of low-income and ELL children (Roberts, 2003; Roberts & Neal, 2004).

One way that you can determine how well the program's monthly goals and standards are meeting children's needs is to consider the percentage of children identified as at-risk at the end of a year of instruction. One program that I worked with used research to identify benchmarks in four categories: high risk, at some risk, age-appropriate achievement, above age-appropriate accomplishment. For each of the assessments administered at the end of the program, the teachers identified scores for cut-offs for each of the four benchmark categories based on what research suggests is at or above the mean for 4-year-olds. For example:

- Children who identified fewer than 13 letters (25 percent or less of the upper- and lowercase alphabet) were considered *at high risk*.

- Children who identified fewer than 26 (50 percent of the alphabet) were considered *at some risk*.

- Children who could identify 26–39 letters (50–75 percent of the alphabet) were considered achieving *at age-appropriate levels*.

- Children who recognized more than 40 letters were considered achieving at *above age-appropriate levels*.

Figure 1.2 presents the benchmarks this particular program established in each of the four categories among several literacy concepts and for a standardized measure of expressive vocabulary. Overall, these benchmarks are quite challenging, especially for children from low-income families who have had few literacy experiences before entering preschool.

Using the benchmarks presented in Figure 1.2, you can identify the number of children who fit under each category at the end of preschool or during a program for 4-year-olds. Figure 1.3 presents the percentage of children from ten preschool classrooms at high risk, at some risk, at age-appropriate levels, and above age-appropriate levels. It is critical to keep

Figure 1.2 Benchmarks Identifying Four Levels of Early Literacy

Domain	High Risk	At Risk	Age-Appropriate	Above Age
Standardized Expressive Vocabulary	70% or less standard score	84–71% standard score	85–100% standard score	above 100% standard score
Alphabet	recognizes less than 25%	recognizes less than 50%	recognizes 50–75%	recognizes more than 75%
Phonemic Awareness		cannot segment beginning phonemes	segments many beginning phonemes	segments all beginning phonemes
Blending Sounds Into Words		blends compound words and syllables segmented by teacher into words	blends words segmented into onset and rime by teacher into words	blends words segmented into phonemes by teacher into words
Concepts About Print		demonstrates book orientation concepts	demonstrates beginning directionality concepts	demonstrates concepts about words and letters
Letter-sound Relationships		knows less than 4 letter–sound relationships	knows 5–8 letter-sound relationships	knows 9–10 letter-sound relationships
Invented Spelling	does not attempt to write words	attempts to write words with random letters	attempts to spell with at least one letter-sound	attempts to spell with two or more letter-sounds
Total Literacy Profile	very low total score on assessment (less than 25%)	low score on assessment (less than 50%)	age-appropriate score on assessment (50–75%)	very high score on assessment (above 75%)

in mind that approximately 80 percent of the children in these classrooms qualified for free or reduced-cost lunch. Given the low levels of literacy achievement generally found in low-income children, the teachers in this project were proud that only 25 percent of their children overall were identified as at risk (and only 10 percent were considered at high risk) at the end of one year of preschool. Most important, 50 percent of the children were identified as achieving above age expectations. In general, teachers in this program were very successful in helping children acquire high levels of alphabet knowledge, phonemic awareness, and letter-sound recognition. They were less successful in helping children achieve high levels of concepts about print and blending onset-rimes and phonemes into words. While invented-spelling scores were low, teachers all felt that having more than 60 percent of the children spell at least three words with one or more appropriate letters was quite an accomplishment. Thus, the teachers agreed the monthly benchmark goals were appropriate, but that they needed to provide more systematic practice with developing concepts about print.

Figure 1.3 Percentage of Children in Five Categories of Early Literacy

Domain	High Risk	At Risk	Age-Appropriate	Above Age	On Target
Standardized Expressive Vocabulary	4%	23%	47%	26%	73%
Alphabet Recognition	6%	9%	12%	73%	85%
Phonemic Awareness		20%	46%	35%	80%
Blending		31%	28%	41%	69%
Concepts/Print		33%	44%	22%	67%
Letter-sound Relationships		26%	20%	54%	74%
Invented Spelling	18%	19%	25%	44%	63%
Total Literacy	10%	15%	25%	50%	75%

Summary

Monthly goals provide guidelines for literacy instruction that are useful in determining which activities to use from your curriculum. These goals indicate outcomes expected for 3- and 4-year-olds in important areas of language and literacy development over the course of a school year. As you observe children's achievement in selected goal areas, you can determine whether you are providing instruction that is sufficiently challenging. I have found that many programs require teachers to document children's growth on far too many standards to be manageable. Consequently, I favor reducing the amount of documentation to a minimum by using monthly goals that highlight foundational language and literacy concepts. The convenience of using monthly goals means that you will have time to meet other expectations required by your programs.

Teachers with whom I worked in the Early Reading First projects were surprised by some of the research that showed what was possible for 3- and 4-year-olds to accomplish. For example, studies have shown that 4-year-olds can identify as many as 75 percent of all alphabet letters. Some of this knowledge is related to their skill in recognizing and writing their own names (Mason, 1980; Worden & Boettcher, 1990; Treiman & Kessler, 2003). Other studies have shown that teaching 3-year-olds to write their names helps them learn alphabet names (Bloodgood, 1999). You may share these teachers' skepticism and question whether many, or even if any, of your children can reach these levels of performance. However, as you strive to transform your language and literacy program, you may want to ask yourself if you are underestimating what preschoolers are capable of achieving.

CHAPTER 2

Transforming the Language and Literacy Environment of the Classroom

The second step in transforming ordinary preschool classrooms into centers of excellence is to transform the classroom environment into a language-rich and print-rich setting. Your primary focus in this transformation process is to identify ways in which you can offer more opportunities for children to use oral language and to encounter and use print in a variety of situations and forms. Through thoughtful planning, you can create a classroom environment that optimizes opportunities for children to use talking, reading, and writing for a range of purposes. The physical resources for reading and writing activities become critical tools for transforming your classroom into a center of learning that offers many beneficial experiences to children.

Classroom Environments Matter

Humans respond to any arranged environment, including classroom settings, in predictable ways. For example, in a setting or context recognized as a bank, people perform certain actions and use certain kinds of language. They make deposits, apply for loans, and make withdrawals using language appropriate to these activities, and perform nonverbal actions such as those required when using an ATM machine. These behaviors and language patterns are consistent across all contexts that are considered banks. Similarly, classroom environments, as behavior settings, have been shown to elicit highly predictable patterns of behavior and language in teachers and children (Fraser, 1991; Weinstein, 1979). Children go to the carpet expecting to participate in whole-group activities such as singing and listening to stories. They go to the home-living center to engage in social dramatic play, and they go to the art center to manipulate materials such as paint and paint brushes. Because classroom environments influence children's behaviors, early childhood professionals have long used design guidelines to create

Research into classroom environments provides insights into how, even with limited resources, you can expand ways to engage children more actively in language and literacy activities. Research reveals the following:

- Some preschool settings do not offer sufficient opportunities for children to talk with adults.

- Teachers can use conversations to deliberately expand selected aspects of children's oral language.

- Children's literacy awareness develops in environments where books and writing materials are readily available to them.

- A variety of props in theme-based dramatic-play centers facilitates children's use of conversation and writing.

- With more books available in the classroom, teachers are more likely to read aloud to children and encourage children to browse through books.

- Modeling writing and displaying children's own writing advances their literacy learning.

- The quality of children's play improves when teachers introduce a variety of materials and model possible roles children might play.

effective classrooms for young children (Harms, Clifford, & Cryer, 1998). These guidelines dictate appropriate arrangement of the classroom space, the nature of the daily schedule, and the nature of interactions between adults and children.

Classrooms Should Be Divided Into Defined Play Spaces

To meet typical early childhood classroom design guidelines, I recommend that you use shelves and other pieces of furniture to create small, defined play spaces usually called centers. Because they are small and intimate, these spaces inhibit children from running around and provide opportunities for interactions among children. When materials are close at hand and readily visible, children are more likely to extend their play and exploration of materials, rather than randomly roam about the room.

Design guidelines suggest that the most effective centers are large enough (75 to 100 square feet) for 3 or 4 children to play together; to accommodate the play of 18–20 children, six to eight centers are needed in each classroom. Each center needs appropriate furniture, such as a table and chairs or a carpet to facilitate use of the materials in that particular center. In order to use space efficiently, you may have one space serve two or three purposes. For example, in most classrooms, large carpets are used to define whole-group areas, but you may also use the carpet to house a center such as blocks where children need large expanses of floor space on which to build.

Areas in a Typical Preschool Classroom

Early childhood classrooms typically include areas for blocks, art, dramatic play (home living), and small manipulatives (puzzles, sorting materials, and small, table-top blocks) as well as book, writing, and computer centers. They may also include a sand and water table, a music center, and a tool bench. Increasingly, classrooms include areas for math and science. Each of these centers is stocked with a variety of different materials appealing to different interests and developmental levels. Each center has shelves on which to store materials, and those materials change throughout the year. All materials are stored in transparent containers, and shelves have picture and word labels of the materials stored in that location. This facilitates children's independent selection and return of materials.

Classroom Time Should Be Divided Into a Variety of Routine Activities

In addition to space allocation within the classroom environment, you also need to take time allocation into consideration and how children's activities will affect the use of space. Most early childhood teachers create a schedule that provides time for a variety of activities and groupings. Typical schedules include whole-group, small-group, and individual activities (often called center time), as well as time for snacks, lunch, napping, and outside play. Within these schedules are routine activities (sometimes called transitions) that occur on a daily basis, such as cleaning up after center time, going to the bathroom, going to the playground, getting ready to go home, entering the classroom in the morning, and getting ready for the nap.

Design guidelines suggest that each classroom include a poster on which to provide resources for children. Resources are sources of information, inspiration, and help, such as a poster on which the daily schedule is printed along with pictures of children engaging in each activity. Children can refer to the pictures on this chart as a resource, for example, to determine how many more activities remain until it is time to go home. Each center may display several pictures of children using the various kinds of materials found in the center in a variety of creative activities. Such displays capture children's interest and suggest to them new activities.

Adults Should Interact With Children Frequently

Finally, design guidelines specify that teachers should facilitate conversations with and among children throughout the day in a variety of activities. Talking with children, either individually or in small groups, as they play provides opportunities for you to model appropriate language use and provide supportive, positive interactions among children. As you participate in conversations with children in these settings, you can find out about their interests and activities, as well as make observations about their language use. The frequency with which children are engaged in extended conversations is a critical factor in facilitating their language development.

Increasing the Quality of Language in Early Childhood Classrooms

Most early childhood teachers are familiar with these design guidelines, and as a result, research has confirmed that the general quality of classroom environments is more than adequate (Barnett, 2001). However, the quality of support for language and literacy is generally lower than that of the overall environment (Dickinson & Sprague, 2001). Research has shown that many children have few opportunities to talk with adult caregivers or teachers in some child care or preschool settings (Snow, Burns, & Griffin, 1998). In order to accelerate children's language development, teachers must transform the way in which they interact with children to increase the number and quality of interactions they have with individual children, especially in extended conversations.

Increase the Number and Quality of Conversations

With responsibility for large numbers of children, it is a challenge for preschool teachers to find time to talk with individual children. I have found that teachers need to make deliberate plans to have at least one extended conversation with a few different groups of children each day of the week. A systematic approach is to plan to sit and stay with a group of children (five to eight children per day) during center time, snack, or outside play. Sitting and staying means that the teacher will spend lots of time during center activities in just a few locations rather than cruising around the room making sure children have materials they need and are engaged in worthwhile activities (McGee & Richgels, 2003). During snack and other mealtimes, teachers will deliberately sit near a few target children in order to purposefully engage these few children in high-quality conversations (Dickinson & Tabors, 2001). Another way that teachers have deliberately planned for conversation is to place a small talk center in the classroom. This center would have a chair for the teacher and a chair for two children. Children who enter the center may stay for up to 5–10 minutes for a child-selected conversation. Thus, throughout the week, the teacher will be sure to have high-quality conversations with all children in a variety of settings.

The way in which you talk to the children may change as you work through the process of transforming your program. Although you must be careful to keep conversations genuine, you can also use conversations to expand children's language. The most effective way to expand children's syntax is to model using sentence patterns slightly more advanced than those used by children. Another strategy is to *repeat and recast* children's responses (Manning-Dratcoski, & Bobkoff-Katz, 1998). For example, if a child says, "My cat meows," you could reply, "My cat meows, too. He comes up to me and meows very loudly." Questioning, when used occasionally, is another strategy that you can employ to extend children's responses. After a child comments, you can ask a question calling for the child to provide more information in a longer and more complex sentence. For example, if the child comments, "My cat meows," you may ask, "Why does your cat meow?" The child may respond with the extended sentence, "My cat meows to go out." You can also *elaborate* on children's comments by repeating some of the child's own words, but embedding those words in slightly more complex sentence structures and adding a bit more related information. For example, one child asked, "When

Daddy comes home?" and his mother elaborated, "Daddy will come home soon, when it gets dark" (Clay, 1998, p. 8).

Increase Specific Kinds of Language Related to Later Reading Achievement

Teacher Reflection

Pre-kindergarten teacher Ede Wortham shares this observation about having conversations with her children: "I have always thought that breakfast provided some of the best opportunities to listen, converse, and interject new/expanded vocabulary. It seems to be the calm part of the day. The children are occupied eating and conversation just seems to flow. It is difficult sometimes to speak with each child at the table. Breakfast, like a lot of the lessons I teach during the day, gives me a glimpse into the lives of the children and also gives me a chance to do a little informal assessment. The child that takes the milk cartons and makes them into a pattern of blue and purple I know has the concept of patterning. The one that finds "100%" on the juice carton is reading environmental print and making the connection to what we write on the message board on days that all of the children are present at school."

Research has shown that three specific types of language have been linked to later reading achievement: decontextualized talk about non-immediate events, analytical talk, and literary language. These kinds of talk may be considered "school talk." Some preschool children will lack experience with school talk because it may be quite different from the talk they are accustomed to using at home. "Home talk" is contextualized in the sense that it features face-to-face interactions, is often accompanied by direct actions that satisfy an immediate purpose, and is based on shared knowledge and experiences. Consequently, it is important for you to provide opportunities for children to hear and use the language of school talk. Children who have more opportunities to talk about non-immediate events, use analytical talk especially as they talk about books, and practice using literary language are more likely to be better readers (Dickinson & Tabors, 2001; Purcell-Gates, 1990).

Decontextualized Talk

Talk about non-immediate events occurs when children talk about something other than what they are doing or seeing in their current context. When children are asked to describe a past event in which they participated—such as a holiday celebration or a trip to the dentist—they must talk about people and activities that are not in their current context. That is, as speakers discuss past events, they use decontextualized language in which words refer to objects or events outside the immediate context of the speaker and listener. The reason why decontextualized language is so critical to practice is because this is the type of language found in printed texts. When adults help children recount past events, they are preparing children to understand language used in books (Dickinson & Smith, 1994; Purcell-Gates, 1988). Talk centers are a great opportunity for you to chat with one or two children about their past experiences. By engaging your children in talk about non-immediate events, you can learn a great deal about individual children and their lives outside the classroom.

Analytical Talk

Analytical talk is language used to reason and explain (Dickinson & Smith, 1994). This kind of language is used when children engage in higher-level thinking and is characteristic of academic achievement. In preschool, children are more likely to engage in this kind of talk when they discuss books: why a character in a book acted as he did, what the character was feeling, and what the character might do next. You can foster analytical talk by taking time to reread a story in the book center to a small group of children and engage them in conversation about the book.

Literary Language

Literary language is the specific kind of language patterns and vocabulary that are found in books rather than in everyday conversations (Purcell-Gates, 1988). Literary language includes varied word order (such as *out the gate they went* or *our mittens we have found*) and sophisticated vocabulary (such as *golden slippers* or *feast*). In order to increase children's use of literary language, you can read books aloud more frequently. Researchers have also found that props are effective in prompting children to dramatize or retell stories (Purcell-Gates, McIntyre, & Freppon, 1990). Adding costumes and other props to the home-living area are other resources you can provide to encourage children to act out stories.

The design guidelines that I have outlined and suggestions for increasing oral language interactions will only help teachers reach the first step: creating environments that are language-rich. Additional guidelines are needed to reach the second step: creating print-rich environments.

Transforming the Classroom Environment: Becoming Print-Rich

Research on the nature of what can be called print-rich homes and pre-schools prompted other researchers to investigate the effects of transforming classrooms into print-rich environments. For example, researchers added theme-based dramatic-play centers, such as a post office or a doctor's office, and props that could prompt pretend reading and writing such as appointment cards or patient charts (Morrow & Rand, 1991; Neuman & Roskos, 1993). Researchers found that these children made more attempts to pretend to read and write using these dramatic-play props. Other researchers added more books to the classrooms. These researchers found that with more books available in the classroom, teachers were more likely to read aloud to children and to provide more frequent opportunities for children to browse through books (Neuman, 1999).

Print-Rich Homes and Their Role

A number of years ago, researchers discovered that a few children learned to read and write before they entered school (Durkin, 1966; Clark, 1976). The researchers wondered how these children had accomplished this feat when their parents claimed they had not taught their children to read. They found that these children lived in homes filled with books, paper, pencils, crayons, and other writing tools. They found that these preschoolers frequently pretended to read and write (Teale, 1978; Taylor & Dorsey-Gaines, 1988), and were surrounded by adults who read and wrote and provided children with books and writing tools.

Researchers concluded that the children's home environment influenced the children's reading and writing behaviors. These boys and girls had access to an abundance and variety of tools to spark reading and writing, and they had access to adults who modeled reading and writing. In such print-rich environments, adults frequently encouraged children to read and write and provided support as they did so. The result is that children who have access to books and writing materials at home and opportunities to see adults reading and writing will begin to emulate these behaviors. These experiences enable children to develop interest in literacy and acquire some preliminary understandings about print.

Research has also shown that some preschools have the same characteristics of print-rich homes. In these settings, teachers model reading and writing and provide opportunities for children to engage in reading and writing with teachers and in their pretend play (Cochran-Smith, 1984; Rowe, 1998).

Researchers have also trained adults to be more effective as they interact with children in these print-enriched environments. For example, child care workers increased the number of interactions they had with children while reading aloud when they were taught how to use high-quality literature (Neuman, 1999). Training adults to interact with children in print-enriched dramatic-play centers also resulted in children having more extended concepts about literacy (Neuman & Roskos, 1993). Training teachers to model writing is another method that has resulted in higher literacy achievement for children. In classrooms in which there are multiple displays of children's own emergent writing and of the teachers' modeling of writing for a variety of purposes, children's literacy concepts are more advanced than in classrooms in which teachers do not display models of writing (Taylor, Blum, & Logsdon, 1986).

Research with slightly older children has revealed that the design and contents of book centers matter: well-designed book centers encourage children to visit the center more frequently, to stay longer, and to browse through and talk about books more frequently. When adults sit and stay in book centers more frequently, children are more likely to engage in analytical talk and to practice using literary language.

The Need for Transformation

Most early childhood teachers believe that their classrooms are language- and print-rich. They often describe to me how much talk goes on in their classrooms. Most of these teachers feel as if they talk, talk, talk from the moment the first child enters the classroom until the last child leaves. When I visit these classrooms, I am struck by the buzz of children talking, sometimes quite loudly. I often note displays of children's drawings, posters, and photographs that are readily visible in these colorful, busy preschool classrooms.

On closer inspection, however, I have found, despite many teachers' beliefs, that most classrooms provide only a basic level of support for language and literacy development. I have used a popular assessment tool, the Literacy

The components of a well-designed library center (Fractor, Woodruff, Martinez, & Teale, 1993) include:

- space large enough for three or four children (25 square feet per child) and the teacher
- soft, comfortable seating
- at least 100 books (a total of five times the number of children in the classroom; however, not all books should be stored in the library center)
- adequate shelves and other containers to hold 25–30 books for easy access by children
- some books displayed on shelves that allow covers to face outward
- some books that rotate in and out of the center
- a listening center with equipment for at least two children to listen to recorded books
- attractive wall displays

Environment Checklist of the ELLCO Early Language and Literacy Classroom Observation Toolkit (Smith & Dickinson, 2002) to measure the level of support that many preschool classroom environments provide for literacy development. The Literacy Environment Checklist includes 24 items with a possible total of 41 points. The authors developed this checklist to reflect a set of characteristics that could be expected to facilitate extended explorations of reading and writing. Thus, the checklist includes items that assess whether classrooms have a well-designed book and writing center, whether there are indications that teachers deliberately plan instruction that includes modeling of writing and reading aloud to children, and whether children's writing is displayed. I have used this tool to evaluate the quality of several dozen preschool classroom environments.

In general, I have found that most classrooms received a score of 10–22 on the 41-point scale. It is a rare classroom that received a score above 20. Most teachers arranged their classrooms so that a book center was available to children, and they did stock plenty of books in places that were accessible to children. Some teachers had writing centers, alphabet puzzles, and listening centers. Few teachers had enough variety of books at different levels of difficulty. Almost no teachers had appropriate books, writing utensils, and props to encourage pretend reading and writing throughout various centers. None provided a print-enriched, themed dramatic-play area other than the home-living center.

Once I shared these results with teachers, they were eager to learn more about the specific characteristics and components of a high-quality, print-rich environment. As one teacher put it, "Everyone knows to put in a book center and have plenty of books. If I know what else my children need, I'll make sure it gets there." Most teachers were confident that with information about what ought to be included in the classroom, they could make the necessary adjustments. In the next section, I describe characteristics and components that define high-quality language and literacy environments.

Components and Characteristics of Literacy-Rich Environments

Figure 2.1 presents a list of the characteristics and components that define a high-quality literacy-rich environment. This list is presented in the form of a checklist, similar to the Literacy Environment Checklist from ELLCO

(Smith & Dickinson, 2002). You can use it to evaluate the quality of your preschool classroom environment. The list includes six major components:

- book center
- writing center
- reading and writing around the classroom
- themed dramatic-play center
- classroom displays
- the teacher's role

Teachers I have worked with use this list to self-assess how well they have stocked and arranged their classrooms. When transforming classroom environments, I have found that teachers generally start by rearranging and adding materials to their book and writing centers.

The book and writing areas should be separate, large centers devoted only to reading and writing or related activities. They should have appropriate furniture, such as soft seating for reading and a large table for writing. They should have an abundance and variety of materials, including books of varying levels of difficulty and representing different genres, and a variety of writing instruments and papers. Displays should provide children with models for reading and writing activities within the center. Most teachers find it relatively easy to adjust their classrooms to accommodate larger, better-stocked book and writing centers.

Book Center

Figure 2.1 Language and Literacy Environment Checklist: Preschool

Directions: Observe in the classroom without children present.

Book Center

Physical Characteristics

_____ Separated into nook (with shelves on at least 2 sides)

_____ Devoted only to books and other book-related activities

_____ At least one shelf in which book covers are displayed facing outward

_____ Additional shelving or containers (such as plastic crates)

_____ Soft comfortable seating (such as pillows or a couch)

_____ Large enough for 3–4 children (75 square feet or more) and teacher

_____ Books that are generally orderly

_____ Books that are accessible (children can easily pull books from shelves)

_____ Center is accessible (easily entered by children)

Materials

_____ At least 30 or more books displayed

_____ Two or more books that have 1–2 words per page

_____ Two or more books that have 1–2 lines of text per page

_____ Two or more books that have 1–2 paragraphs per page

_____ Five or more award-winning books

_____ Two or more alphabet books

_____ Two or more concept books (e.g., counting, colors, shapes)

_____ Two or more nonfiction books

_____ Three or more predictable books

_____ Materials or display that arouses interest in center (e.g., objects or dolls related to a book, display basket with books teacher has read aloud, pictures of children reading, retelling props)

Writing Center

Physical Characteristics

_____ Separated into nook

_____ Devoted only to writing (e.g., does not share materials, storage, or furniture with art area)

_____ Large enough for at least 2 children and teacher

_____ Center is accessible (easily entered)

Materials

_____ At least three different kinds of writing implements, not including crayons

_____ At least two alternative tools for writing, such as letter stamps, letters to cut, letter sponges, letter tiles

_____ At least three different kinds of materials to write on, such as a whiteboard, lined and unlined paper, notebooks, paper cut in shapes

_____ Alphabet visible to children

_____ Word cards available and visible to children

_____ Models for writing letters available (traceable letters, stencils, directions for letter formation, sandpaper letters)

_____ Models for writing texts available, such as newspapers, magazines, teacher-written samples

_____ Models of written texts such as birthday cards or menus

_____ Displays of children's writing books and writing in use around the room

continued . . .

Books and Writing Around the Classroom

_____ Total number of books available to children is five times number of children

_____ At least five books displayed related to theme

_____ At least five nonfiction books available

_____ At least three related books located in the blocks area

_____ At least three related books located in the dramatic-play area

_____ At least three related books each located in two centers (not book center)

_____ At least one play object to suggest writing in home-living area and one other center, such as a telephone to encourage taking telephone messages, lumber advertisements to encourage making a lumber order for the blocks area

_____ At least one writing tool or implement and materials in home-living area or other center, such as telephone message pad, or lumber order form; cannot be blank paper only

_____ Writing prompts and tools located in close proximity to other center materials

_____ Listening center accessible to children (children must be able to access without adult assistance)

_____ Props for dramatizing or retelling two or more stories, accessible to children

_____ Two or more alphabet puzzles accessible to children

_____ One or more word puzzles or games accessible to children

_____ Display of children's names visible to children

Themed Dramatic-Play Center
(should be in addition to home-living center)

_____ Theme obvious (e.g., grocery store, post office, beauty shop)

_____ At least two play objects or displays to suggest reading; e.g., for a beauty shop: hair magazines, books about hair, posters of hair designs

_____ At least four writing materials, such as appointment book, appointment cards, checkbooks, sign-in register, receipt book

_____ Three or more books related to the theme

_____ Display of at least three children's writing

_____ Display of at least two teacher models of writing

_____ Reading and writing tools and materials that are visible and accessible to children

_____ Reading and writing materials that are authentic (e.g., would actually be used in a beauty shop)

_____ Reading and writing materials that are located in logical place for use

Displays

_____ Six or more models of writing by the teacher (writing done with children as children observe; can include models in themed drama center); may include shared-writing charts

_____ One or more shared-writing charts

_____ Individual dictation from children or children's writing attempts

_____ Displays of different formats of writing, such as calendar in home-living center, hardware catalogs or advertisements in block center

_____ Six or more displays of materials for read-alouds (e.g., materials read to and with children; must be obvious that the material is read frequently) such as

continued . . .

- Big Books
- Theme books
- Charts of poems or songs
- Daily message
- Books for daily read-aloud (e.g., displayed to be read today)

_____ Displays of children's writing in three or more centers

_____ Display of children's writing includes three or more different kinds of writing, such as telephone message, grocery list, ABC practice, scribble writing, sign-in sheet, writing as a part of small-group instruction

Teacher's Role

_____ Teacher's lesson plans have indications that he/she:

- Targets children for daily conversations
- Plans to model use of reading and writing materials

_____ As the teacher interacts with children during center time, he/she:

- Engages children in extended (longer than 8 turns) conversations
- Engages children in very extended (longer than 20 turns) conversations
- Engages children in non-immediate talk
- Uses sophisticated vocabulary in conversations
- Plays along with children in dramatic play demonstrating reading and writing
- Reads aloud to children in the book center
- Writes with children in the writing center
- Seeks out target children where they are playing to engage them in conversations

Adapted from Literacy Environment Checklist *(Smith & Dickinson, 2002)*

The chart below lists the components of well-stocked book and writing centers.

Components of Effective Book and Writing Centers

	Writing Center	Book Center
Space	• sectioned into center for only writing	• sectioned into center for only reading
Furniture	• table large enough for 2–3 children and teacher • table of height for children • shelves to hold materials	• area large enough for 3–4 children and teacher • soft pillows, carpet • some shelves with covers facing outward
Materials	• variety of writing instruments • variety of paper and surfaces	• variety of books • variety of printed materials
Displays	• children's and teacher's writing	• photographs of children reading
Other	• alphabet puzzles, print samples • word cards, alphabet display	• retelling props (toys related to books, stuffed toys to read to)

The writing center provides a place where you can interact with children as they write or pretend to write. You can model deciding what to write, selecting materials, and talking with children about their writing. As children talk about their writing, you can ask questions to further children's concepts. For example, you might ask, "Are you writing a list or a message?" Or, "Who are you writing the message to? How will you send your message?" You may invite children to read their writing, but be prepared when children decline or say, "I'm just writing." Your role is to help children accomplish what they are attempting to do rather than to tell them how and what to write. Most important, avoid correcting children's writing or insisting on standard letter formation. Rather, you can pretend right along with children and engage in the kind of writing they are using—of course, they may sometimes demonstrate more conventional

Writing Center

Teacher Reflection

Ede Wortham shared these observations about what happened in her classroom when she introduced an additional themed dramatic-play center: "The dramatic-play center, which is a 'garden center,' has been a big hit with the children. They have been writing lots of orders and charging exorbitant amounts of money for their creations! Of all the Early Reading First project extras I had to do in my classroom, the addition of the second dramatic-play center was the one I resisted the most. It was one more thing to get together and one more thing to clean up. The payoff has been the language and writing that has been a result of the additional center. The children have had many more opportunities to expand their vocabulary, and the writing from this area has been some of the most creative I have received."

writing as well. (See photo for an example of a good writing center.) The purpose of the writing center is to provide opportunities for children to engage in writing at their own level for their own purposes so that they begin to develop understanding of how writing can be used to communicate. The way in which you talk with children about their writing can foster their interest in writing and their willingness to talk about their writing in personal, rather than academic, terms.

The Need for Themed Dramatic-Play Centers

Dramatic play is a particularly rich context for supporting preschool children's language and literacy explorations (Snow, Burns, & Griffin, 1998). Nearly every early childhood classroom includes a home-living dramatic-play center, and it is a favorite choice activity for most children. This is not surprising because dramatic-play centers encourage children to take on different roles in authentic activities. Because of their own experiences, children are familiar with the roles of "mom," "dad," "grandma," and "visitor."

However, play in the home-living center, even when it is enriched with reading and writing props, is not enough to stimulate pretend reading and writing beyond children's current experiences. Children need to be challenged to take on additional roles found in their communities. They can become clerks in flower shops, beauticians, managers of fast-food restaurants, and TV weather persons when additional themed dramatic-play centers are placed in the classroom. Therefore, print-rich classrooms include a second dramatic-play center in addition to the home-living dramatic-play area. For example, Figures 2.2 and 2.3 present several samples of children's writing in a variety of dramatic-play centers including the home-living center. Figure 2.2 is an appointment card created in a beauty/barbershop, and Figure 2.3 is a time card used in a doughnut shop.

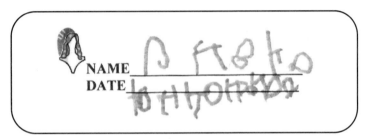

Figure 2.2 *Appointment card created in a beauty/barbershop*

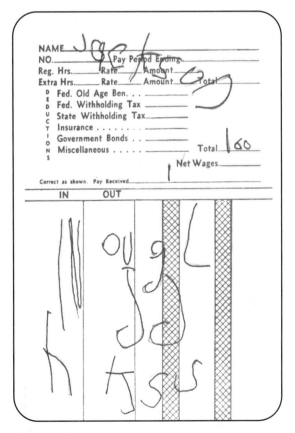

Figure 2.3 *Time card used in a doughnut shop*

Most teachers struggle with finding space in their classrooms to place a second dramatic-play center. However, they have found that the quality of children's play dramatically increases when they introduce these centers. Figure 2.4 (page 44) presents the floor plan of one classroom before it was transformed into a high-quality language- and print-rich environment. This floor plan shows that with small adjustments, the furniture arrangement could be optimal for creating nooks separated from the remainder of the classroom. Initially, there was a large empty space, and the reading center was woefully small.

Figure 2.5 (page 45) presents the floor plan of the same classroom after small but dramatic changes. Now the centers are well defined, and the book center is prominently located and sufficiently large to entice children to enter. There is a second dramatic-play center (a market) that has been located near the home-living area. The teacher has more room in the whole-group area and a place close at hand to store materials for lessons. After this transformation, the teacher reported that children were more likely to play in various locations around the classroom, where before conflicts easily arose because so many children wanted to play either in the home-living area or in the block area. Now the teacher and children play together in their enriched home-living center as well as in other locations in the classrooms

Teachers report that having a second dramatic-play center allows children to choose to play in the more familiar home-living area, but also to play in a new pretend community setting, such as a TV station. Having both centers allows pretend weather persons to get up, get ready to go to work, drive to work, give the weather report, and go back home to dinner. Thus, children can move between centers and extend the "scripts" of their play into highly complex play episodes. In fact, one of the goals of the second dramatic-play center is to enrich the quality of children's play as well as to provide new models of reading and writing.

High-Quality Play Includes . . .

- Extended scripts organized into several related play episodes (e.g., getting dressed for work, driving to work, giving a weather report, fixing and eating dinner)
- Authentic reading (e.g., pretending to read a weather map, pretending to read a newspaper after dinner, pretending to read a telephone book to look up a telephone number)
- Authentic writing (e.g., writing a pretend weather map, writing the temperature, writing a pretend telephone message)
- Negotiating with and engaging others in the play scripts (e.g., engaging another child to be the reporter on location or a camera person)
- Negotiating the content and direction of the play with others (e.g., being willing to trade off being the weather person, deciding whether a hurricane is arriving now or later)

Kay Armstrong invites children to write invitations for a birthday party.

Encouraging High-Quality Play in Themed Dramatic-Play Centers

High-quality play emerges when teachers introduce materials to children and when they model possible roles children might play (Bodrova & Leong, 1998). Using these resources, you can also model appropriate authentic reading and writing activities and demonstrate how to act, read, and write in the center. You can invite children to add reading and writing activities to their ongoing play.

The description of a flower shop as a dramatic-play center on pages 46 and 47 shows how teachers can slowly introduce more roles and more complex scripts while gradually adding more complex reading and writing activities. It also illustrates several guidelines for themed dramatic-play centers (Roskos & Neuman, 2001).

An abundance of reading and writing props and materials should be visible and accessible to children so that they are encouraged to participate in a range of reading and writing activities. Children will not remember to read a garden catalog to plan a garden unless prompted by garden catalogs. When one child looks at a garden catalog, others will want to do so. When one child writes a price tag, others will want to do so. Children will be happy writing price tags for many minutes and use up lots of materials.

The reading and writing materials need to be varied so that they serve a variety of different purposes. In the flower shop, the teacher prepared check books and receipt forms. Additionally, she could have prepared inventory forms on which children could tally the number of pots, trowels, and flowers.

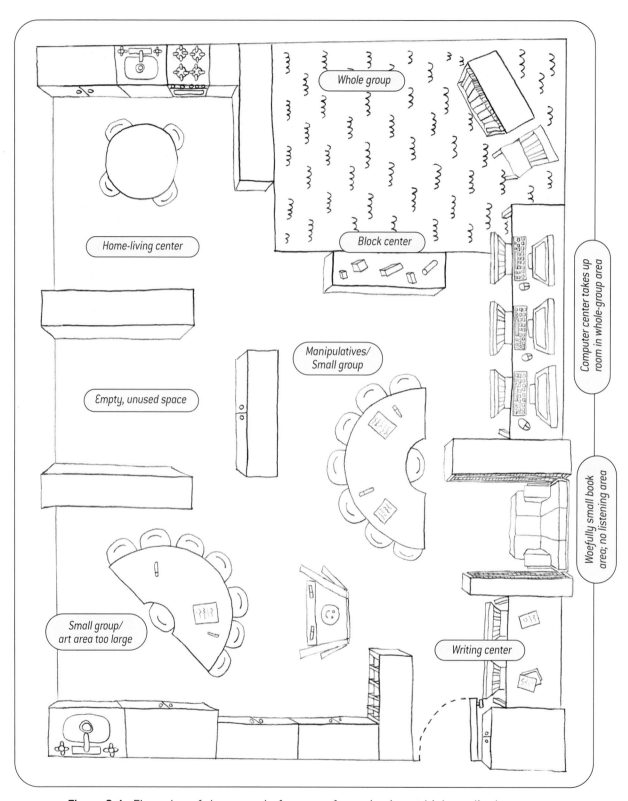

Figure 2.4 *Floor plan of classroom before transformation into a high-quality language- and print-rich environment*

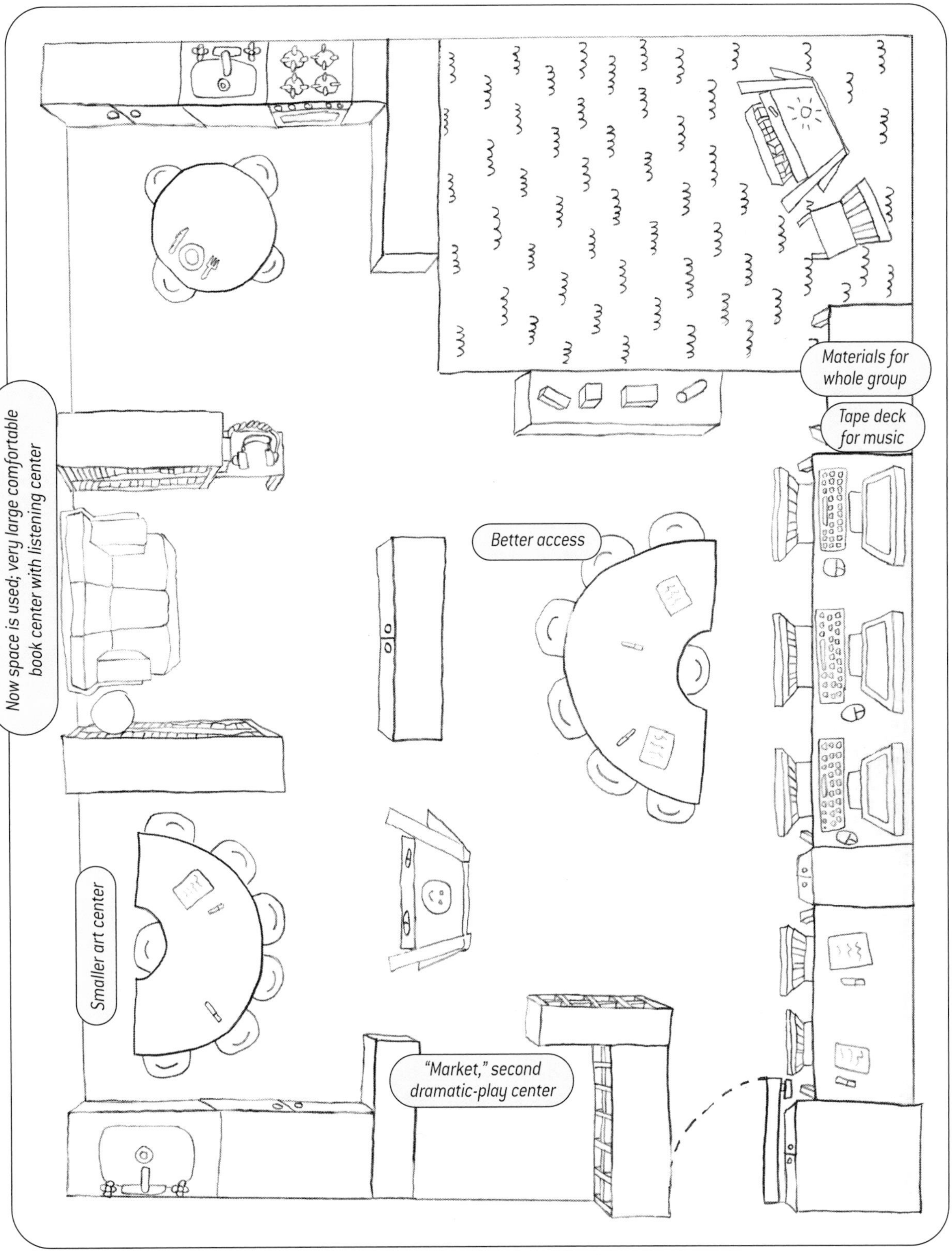

Materials for whole group
Tape deck for music
Better access
Now space is used; very large comfortable book center with listening center
Smaller art center
"Market," second dramatic-play center

Figure 2.5 *Floor plan of classroom after transformation*

An Example of a Second Dramatic-Play Center in a Preschool Classroom

The teacher noticed that in the flower shop she set up as the second dramatic-play center in her classroom, most children merely manipulated the props. They filled pots with small stones using trowels and planted plastic flowers in the pots. She modeled pretending to buy flowers and writing a check, then modeled writing a receipt. Children added these activities to their play scripts. However, this teacher wanted the children to do much more.

In order to increase the quality of the children's play, the teacher realized that she had to be more systematic in considering possible roles for the flower shop and possible authentic reading and writing activities people actually do in those roles. In the initial stages of using the flower shop, she had intuitively modeled the role of flower shop customer and flower shop clerk. After considering these two roles more carefully, she identified additional activities of customers and clerks. She helped the children realize that customers read price tags, signs, and advertisements; they write checks, sign credit card slips, and count money. Similarly, she modeled clerks' activities—writing price tags, signs, and receipts. Of course, these new roles led to the addition of more props such as large sheets of paper to prompt writing signs and small slips of paper to prompt writing price tags, receipt books, and thank-you cards.

Because the children were not familiar with flower shops and ordering flower arrangements, the teacher knew that she would have to model many of these activities. She had many options that she could model for the children—for example, shopping for a flower arrangement for a wedding, birthday, or seasonal holiday. In addition, she could model other roles for clerks, such as inviting "customers" to write a card for their arrangements.

Flower shop manager is another role that the teacher could have added to the flower shop center. Managers write advertisements, prepare catalogs and send them to customers, take inventory, and order new goods for their shops. These new roles suggest new reading and writing activities: reading competitors' advertisements, writing advertisements, creating catalogs, writing

continued . . .

envelopes, making a list of current stock, and reading catalogs to buy new stock. Obviously, to carry out these roles, the teacher would need to add more props to the center: flower advertisements from the newspaper, magazines, and telephone book; inventory forms; flower catalogs; large envelopes and other materials to make catalogs and advertisements. Children would need to see models of these roles and reading and writing in action. The teacher could model a new activity, such as pretending to read a flower advertisement in the newspaper and deciding to shop for flowers for a birthday present, for about three or four minutes each morning during whole-group time over the next week. Throughout the week she could demonstrate reading a phone book to locate a florist to buy a flower arrangement for Mother's Day, looking through a catalog of flower seeds to decide what to plant in her garden, and how to take inventory and order new stock. These demonstrations would allow her to make sure all children become more familiar with scripts for play in the flower shop. She would also continue to visit the flower shop for at least part of center time over the next two weeks.

She could also have prepared small note cards for children to write messages to accompany their flower arrangements.

The materials in the center need to be located in close proximity to where children are most likely to use them and in containers that children can access easily. For example, the teacher used a shelf to make a counter for the flower shop on which she placed the receipt forms and checkbooks. She could have placed a small desk for the manager's office, on which she might have arranged inventory forms, a telephone book, and an order form.

As you transform your dramatic-play centers, you can make sure all of these reading and writing materials are both authentic and useful for children's play by modeling a "script" using the reading and writing materials. Reading and writing materials that you select may be used later in other themed centers. For example, receipts and checkbooks are appropriate for restaurants and beauty shops as well as the flower shop. Thus, children develop a growing repertoire of reading and writing pretend-play scripts that they can apply to other themed play settings.

Classroom Displays

Classroom displays can offer a first-time visitor to your classroom some immediate insights into the kinds of activities in which the children are engaged. The materials you place on walls, shelves, or bulletin boards provide evidence of children's work as well as the range of learning experiences offered. To ensure that the displays continue to attract children's attention and contribute to their learning, you should develop a plan for systematically changing the displays.

Three kinds of displays are needed in print-rich classrooms: displays that are the result of teacher modeling of writing for different purposes, displays that reflect the materials used in reading aloud to children, and displays of children's writing. The most effective displays are those produced by you and your children rather than those obtained commercially.

Models of Writing

During shared writing, teachers model writing for a variety of functions. (See Chapter 4 for more information about creating shared-writing charts for classroom display.) In shared writing, you write as children contribute ideas for the content. You can model recording information in various forms, such as writing directions for making a sponge painting of the ocean, making a list of the animals that children saw on a field trip to the zoo, or writing a list of predictions children have made about an experiment mixing different colors of paint. Because shared-writing experiences are intended to extend children's language, you should strive to include sophisticated vocabulary in some of the charts. These charts can be placed on the classroom walls. You may want to create a large scrapbook to hold charts that you no longer want to display.

The most effective displays of teacher's writing are useful to children, are accessible to and used by children, and are fresh. For ideas about useful charts, see the examples in the sidebar.

Examples of Writing Displays

- A chart of all the children's names with their photographs is something that children can use for a variety of activities; for example, they may identify their own name, identify classmates' names, identify letters, count the number of pictures, or count the number of boys and the number of girls.

- A chart on which the teacher has written a message can be expanded when children are invited to add their ideas to it. This chart might be a large birthday card to which all the children sign their names. It might also be a list of things children saw on a field trip, or a calendar on which children can add drawings and words to describe the weather each day.

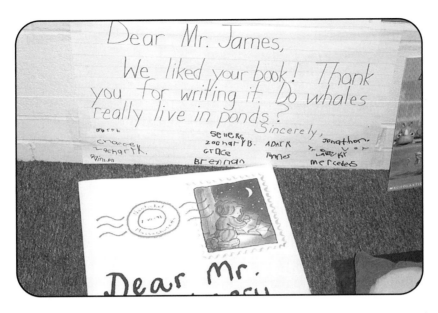

A shared-writing letter to the author of Dear Mr. Blueberry *signed by all the children*

Changing the displays of teachers' writing as themes change keeps the displays fresh and interesting to children. The following is a summary of the characteristics of highly effective displays.

Book Displays

Displays should always include books and texts that you read aloud to children frequently. Some examples of such displays include a collection of Big Books, a basket of books by a favorite author, a shelf on which several books related to a common theme are displayed, and a chart stand with poems and nursery rhymes. The books and texts on display should reflect a variety of difficulty levels: texts with one or two words, some with one or two lines of print, and some with one or two paragraphs of text. Books and other texts should include a variety of genres including folktales, realistic stories, information books, how-to books, biographies, fantasy, and poetry.

Tips for Making Children's Writing Visible

One teacher I have worked with keeps a collection of colored tape in a special classroom location. When children write, they are invited to use the tape to hang their writing in a location of their choice. Another teacher invites children who have written anything during center time to place the writing on her rocking chair. When center time is over, she takes a few minutes to show each piece of writing and acknowledge the children's activities. It is not surprising that writing is a frequent activity in these two classrooms.

Characteristics of High-Quality Displays

Displays of modeled writing activities should:

- Have a purpose
- Demonstrate writing for different purposes
- Extend children's concepts and language
- Be useful to children
- Be accessible to and used by children
- Be fresh

Displays of read-aloud activities should:

- Demonstrate a connection (such as a relationship to a common topic or theme)
- Represent a variety of difficulty levels
- Represent a variety of genres
- Be accessible to children
- Be fresh

Displays of children's writing should:

- Be located in proximity to where they were written
- Reflect a variety of different kinds of writing
- Be representative of all children in the classroom
- Be fresh

There should be an obvious way in which children get access to books that teachers read aloud. You may place a basket labeled "Daily Read-Aloud" near the chart stand or easel or inside the book center. Children will know where the basket is located so they can browse through the books during center time. To keep children interested in the books and other print materials, you should plan to change the displays as themes change.

Annie Walker and Katesha Washington share a story about a plump bear.

Children's Writing

Children are usually delighted to see displays of their own writing in the classroom. Such displays, if changed frequently, help sustain children's motivation to write and help you observe their writing behaviors. Displays of children's writing are best located in proximity to where children created them: lumber orders in the blocks area, grocery lists in the home-living center, and pretend stories in the writing center. Displays of children's writing should reflect the level of writing of all children in the classroom. Some children will be scribbling, others writing with letter-like symbols, and others copying words. Similarly, writing that is displayed should reflect the variety of writing children produce.

The Teacher's Role in Language- and Print-Rich Classrooms

As I described earlier in this chapter, a language-rich classroom environment is one in which teachers utilize time in the daily schedule to talk in extended conversations with individual children (such as at a talk center or during snack, lunch, and outside play). If you develop a deliberate plan for talking with individual children on particular days, you will ensure that all children have an opportunity to engage in conversations (rather than merely the vocal children). In conversations with your children, you can use sophisticated vocabulary to help them expand their own vocabularies and you can repeat, recast, and elaborate on their talk to provide them with models of effective language. Talking with children in a variety of situations enables you to help them understand the kinds of talk that occur in school: decontextualized talk, analytical talk, and literary talk. The chart below presents a summary of teachers' roles in extending children's language development.

Teacher's role in expanding children's language development:

- Engage individual children in frequent, extended conversations
- Use sophisticated vocabulary
- Use strategies such as repeating, recasting, elaborating, and questioning to extend children's responses in conversations
- Talk about non-immediate events and activities
- Prompt analytical talk about books (predict, explain, infer)
- Plan a predictable routine to insure conversations with each child

Teacher's role in expanding children's literacy engagements:

- Model authentic uses of reading and writing in themed play activities
- Provide abundant and varied reading and writing materials
- Encourage children to pretend to read and write
- Acknowledge the value of children's pretend reading and writing
- Interact with children in a supportive, positive manner as they attempt to read and write

A print-rich classroom contains an abundance of reading and writing materials that you can use to model how and why they are used for authentic purposes. You can encourage children to pretend to read and write by joining in their play and by modeling how to read and write in their play scripts. By displaying many different examples of all children's writing, you are acknowledging and valuing their efforts. You can support and extend children's writing attempts by visiting the writing center and asking children about their activities. You can support children's reading by visiting the book center frequently and helping children retell favorite books or reread books. The chart above also summarizes the teacher's role in extending children's literacy development.

Transforming the Classroom Environment

Transforming the classroom environment will not happen overnight. You need time to select new resources and to plan how to model the use of the new materials. Furthermore, children need time to adjust to changes. In the same way that you approach planning for your lessons, you can develop a systematic plan for transforming your classroom. Here is a plan that a group of teachers used to successfully transform their classroom environments.

A Practical Plan for Transforming the Classroom Environment

First, we focused on the book center and evaluated the number and quality of books as well as the physical arrangement of furniture. We added books and rearranged the location and layout of this center to meet all the criteria listed in Figure 2.1. We usually did this before school started so that children would be familiar with this center from the very first. At the same time, we focused on the writing center following the same steps. We made sure that these two centers were well stocked with materials before children entered the classrooms, and during the first few days of school, we modeled how to use the materials in each center. During these first few days, we were careful to display some models of our own writing in the writing center to remind children of possible activities in that center.

Over the first two weeks of school, we began to deliberately display a growing collection of books and other texts that we used for read-aloud. We placed a basket in the book center labeled "Teacher Read-Aloud" and another basket under the easel labeled "Daily Read-Aloud." We placed books that we planned to read aloud in the basket under the easel, and after reading a given book, we placed it in the basket in the book center. We put the book in the basket before center time and reminded children that the book would be available in the book center. We displayed nursery rhymes and finger plays and read them almost daily. We decided on a location to display a supply of books related to the current theme.

We also began displaying our own models of writing. One of the first models of writing that one of us created was a list of boys (then of girls) in the classroom. This teacher glued pictures of each child on a chart before beginning to write with the children, and then she asked each child to say the first letter of his or her name as she wrote. Another teacher was

continued . . .

teaching colors during the first month of school, so she modeled writing a class favorite-color tally starting with the color red. She wrote the following question before beginning the activity with the children: "Is red your favorite color?" After reading the title, all the children had an opportunity to respond. Then she described how to fill in the tally graph. She had prepared sticky notes on which she had written each child's name and placed them on the easel beside the tally graph. At center time, she helped children locate their name, remove the sticky, and place it on the graph. Later that day, the children counted the number of "Yes" and "No" responses. Then the teacher wrote two summary sentences: "Red is the favorite color of 7 children. Red is not the favorite color of 2 children." She used this tally form for all the primary and secondary colors. Figure 2.6 shows the tally form.

red is my favorite color						
yes	Ellis	Tykira	Alexa	Haille	MarCadia	Zavarius
					Jackson	
no	Terrell	Stundrick				

Figure 2.6 *Tally Form for "Red is my favorite color"*

After the first few weeks of school, we began infusing reading and writing materials into the home-living and blocks areas. In each of these cases, we modeled writing and using the materials included in the centers during whole-group time. We displayed several models of our own writing in these centers and posted photographs of children pretending to read and write. When children were familiar with these materials, we infused reading and writing materials in two additional centers, again demonstrating their use in play. Finally, we added the second dramatic-play area, and, over a month's time, increased the number and complexity of the reading and writing props. Most of us were able to introduce all the elements listed in Figure 2.1 into our classrooms by the end of the second month of school.

Summary

Language- and print-rich classrooms provide an environment that encourages children to talk and to pretend to read and write in a variety of ways. By building on your existing resources, you can create an environment that invites children to be enthusiastic participants in learning. Obviously, this transformation is going to require planning and time, but you can begin by thinking about a schedule for the changes; for example, you can identify what to do before school begins, within the first two weeks, and within the first two months. You may find it practical to begin with arranging the classroom space to accommodate a book center, a writing center, and a second dramatic-play center. With these centers in place, you can determine resources and displays that will provide a range of opportunities for children to engage in reading and writing activities. The Language and Literacy Environment Checklist shown in Figure 2.1 (pages 34–38) is a useful tool for evaluating and transforming your classroom environment. A classroom that reflects the features on this checklist will provide optimal support for language and literacy development.

CHAPTER 3

Transforming Reading Aloud and Dramatizing Activities Through Embedded Instruction

Reading aloud and dramatizing are among the traditional activities that you likely use frequently in your preschool program. These time-honored practices have been used to introduce children to many new ideas and ways of expression. However, it is possible to use these activities with preschoolers to even greater advantage. Research has revealed that these activities can be enhanced through a variety of techniques that demonstrate to children the purposes for reading and writing. You can use these techniques to augment children's language and literacy experiences by embedding routines that familiarize children with features of books, concepts about print, literary vocabulary, and elaborated talk. Models of elaborated talk enable children to make inferences, thus expanding both their vocabulary and thinking. Such activities in no way detract from the quality of children's enjoyment in listening to and dramatizing stories; rather, they enhance children's learning experiences. These activities are essential factors in transforming preschool instruction so that children have opportunities to experience the language of school, notably decontextualized talk, analytical talk, and literary language.

Characteristics of Purposeful, Embedded Language and Literacy Activities

When you read or write with children to serve a real purpose (for example, reading aloud to enjoy a funny story or writing an enlarged version of a thank-you letter to a class visitor), you are providing them with a meaningful experience from which they learn that reading and writing are valuable tools that will help them in many things in life. For example, you might read aloud a book so children can identify an insect they have collected outside or write an enlarged graph to represent how many children like to eat yogurt. In these activities, you are focusing children's attention on the meaning being constructed and its purpose. However, during these activities, embedded within the larger purpose of finding or recording information, you can also draw children's attention to print. For example, you may demonstrate a comprehension strategy by having children scan the illustrations on each page to look for a picture of the insect they have found. As you write on enlarged charts, you may identify the letters you are writing and encourage children to contribute by naming some of the letters. Thus, each of the activities you use in interactive read-alouds, shared reading, and dramatization do double duty. These activities demonstrate meaningful reading and writing in actual practice while at the same time allowing you to teach foundational literacy skills that children need to learn.

As children gain experience in listening to and talking about books, you will be able to observe how their concepts shift and how their language becomes more like that of adults. Because preschool children have different and unique concepts and experiences, they approach a common activity in ways that are consistent with their understandings and experiences. These "individual differences in preschool children's experiences (stemming largely

Research Supports Embedded Language and Literacy Activities

Repeated interactive read-alouds, shared reading, and drama and retelling are three techniques you can use to provide a systematic approach that maximizes children's vocabulary and oral comprehension. Research validates purposeful, embedded instruction that enables all children, including English language learners, to engage in the activities and find them personally meaningful. Notably, these activities have characteristics that favor children's learning in language- and print-rich environments. These characteristics include:

- Child-centered and open-ended activities that allow children to participate at their own level of knowledge and prior experience

- Models of reading behavior that support children's growing awareness of the purposes of reading

- The use of continuous text, which helps children develop understanding of the structure of stories (e.g., character, problem, and resolution) and of informational selections (e.g., sequence, cause-effect relationships)

- Read-alouds in which children interact with the teacher and classmates by answering questions and making comments or predictions about story characters and events

- Shared reading experiences that enable children to develop concepts of print and begin to recognize and use language patterns

- Opportunities for children to acquire concepts about how print functions, which enables them to be more successful in developing skills associated with beginning reading and writing

- Dramatization activities that help extend children's oral language and facilitate the development of effective comprehension

- Retelling opportunities, so that children can acquire a more fully developed sense of the language found in books

from their different ways of exploring their environments) signal the need for schools to plan and provide for activities in the first year of school which will allow all children to widen the range of their preschool experiences, wherever they are starting from. . . . Each child should be introduced to the school's [language and literacy] program at some level with which he or she can engage" (Clay 1991, p. 44).

Interactive read-alouds and shared reading are open-ended activities in which there are no "right" answers or ways to participate. As you use these activities, you are ensuring that all children can contribute using language that is familiar to them. You can elaborate on the children's language so that they become aware of other forms of expression, including "book language."

The materials that you select for embedded activities should be varied in format and topic. A primary purpose of these activities is to enable children to build their oral expression and oral comprehension. Consequently, you will want to use materials that feature continuous text rather than isolated letters or

Child-Centered Instruction

Embedded instruction is child centered because the activities enable all children to participate, bringing to the activities different levels of knowledge and prior experience. Preschool children vary widely in what they know because of differing experiences within their families, communities, and cultures. Theorists who study children's thinking (e.g., Duckworth, 1996) and language acquisition (e.g., Halliday, 1975) have shown that within the scope of their experiences, children construct their own explanations for how things work in the world and how words can be put together to communicate. For example, very young children may call every animal they see a dog or every man "Daddy." Here is how one 2-year-old used his limited number of words and syntax to communicate that he had spilled his milk: "Michael milk. Michael floor. Sippy cup floor. Michael milk sippy cup on floor" (Schmitt, Askew, Fountas, Lyons, & Pinnell, 2005, p. 46). What is important about these examples is that children form their own concepts and use language in their own ways, and these are quite different from those held or used by adults.

Teacher Reflection

Linda Rodgers reflects on interactive read-aloud activities: "I believe that the interactive read-aloud is a great way to get the quietest and shyest child to interact as we talk about the story. I have read *The Three Billy Goats Gruff* (Stevens, 1995) three or four times, we have role played the story, and we have retold it a couple of times. However, interactive read-aloud gives the quiet, shy child a turn to talk and be a part of the story on his or her terms. We always ask 'why' questions or talk about what they could do differently, but today we discussed having a picnic and what to do on a picnic and what we would eat. I found out that no one in my class had *ever* been on a picnic, so of course, later that week we had a picnic lunch outside. The children remembered the 'goats' grass lunch,' and we discussed the book while we ate our picnic lunch."

sounds. Continuous text includes books, magazines, newspaper want ads, graphs of recorded information, and advertisements, as well as meaningful lists, such as a list of all the children's names, or a grocery list. These materials should make sense and serve purposes that are evident to children. The following summarizes the characteristics of purposeful, embedded language and literacy activities:

Purposeful, embedded language and literacy instruction . . .

- Is focused primarily on meaning in a purposeful activity
- Is child centered in that the activity allows for children to bring to it their unique knowledge and experiences
- Is open-ended in that there is no one prescribed way of participating
- Involves the use of continuous text

The Value of Repeated Interactive Read-Alouds

Reading aloud to young children has a long tradition in early childhood education as a valuable means to expand their vocabulary, language, and concepts (McGee, 2003). There are many different kinds of books that you can choose to read aloud, but it is likely that you use two basic techniques for reading these different books. *Repeated interactive read-aloud* is a technique that you use when you want to help children expand their vocabulary and develop oral comprehension strategies. The other technique, *shared reading*, is used when you want to help children acquire other literacy concepts such as learning about print, rhyming words, alliteration (words with the same beginning phoneme), alphabet recognition, or letter-sound relationships. Of course, all books should be enjoyed, so that during both repeated interactive read-alouds and shared reading techniques you can draw children's attention to meaning.

Research-Based Best Practices for Read-Alouds: The Teacher's Role

Many researchers have attempted to identify the methods of reading aloud that are most effective in enhancing children's vocabulary, language, and oral comprehension (McGee & Schickedanz, 2007). Following are some recent findings:

- The most effective read-alouds for developing language and comprehension are those in which children ask and answer questions or make comments or predictions rather than passively listening (Dickinson, 2001). Such read-alouds are called interactive or dialogic (Whitehurst, et al., 1994; 1999).

- Merely inviting children to comment about book illustrations or events in storybooks does not seem to be sufficient for accelerating their literacy development. Instead, children's growth in

List of Books for Interactive Read-Alouds: Farm Unit

Narrative Fiction

Big Red Barn by M. W Brown

Farmer Duck by M. Waddell

The Pig in a Pond by M. Waddell

Pigsty by M. Teague

Mrs. Wishy-Washy's Farm by J. Cowley

Nonfiction

Farming by G. Gibbons

Where Do Chicks Come From? by A. E. Sklansky

Pattern Books

Big Fat Hen by K. Baker

Fiddle-I-Fee by W. Hillenbrand

Alphabet Books

G Is for Goat by P. Palacco

Folktales for Drama

Little Red Hen by P. Galdone

Narrative Fiction

Knuffle Bunny by M. Willems

Matthew and Tilly by R. C. Jones

No, David! by D. Shannon

Oonga Boonga: Big Brother's Magic Words by F. Wishinsky

Peter's Chair by E. J. Keats

Do Like a Duck Does! by J. Hindley

Nonfiction

How a House Is Built by G. Gibbons

Building a House by B. Barton

Pattern Books

Hush!: A Thai Lullaby by M. Ho

Where Is My Baby? by H. Ziefert

Alphabet Books

The Alphabet Book by P. D. Eastman

Folktales for Drama

Henny Penny by P. Galdone

The Three Billy Goats Gruff by J. Stevens

comprehension and vocabulary is related to how frequently they engage in analytical talk (Dickinson & Smith, 1994).

- The rich vocabulary found in sophisticated storybooks and nonfiction can be used to extend children's language and vocabulary (Collins, 2005).

- Research has shown that as effective readers listen to a story, they frequently call to mind the story's problem and consider events in relation to this problem (Van den Broek, 2001).

- Good readers intuitively try to figure out a story's problem. However, young children find story problems challenging because they are not usually directly stated in stories (Paris & Paris, 2003; Van den Broek,

1994), and young children naturally seem to focus on characters and their actions (Benson, 1997; Stein & Glenn, 1979).

These research findings offer guidance for techniques that you can use to transform your approach to read-alouds. You can model analytical talk by elaborating on children's responses to questions and using the phrase "I'm thinking . . ." to scaffold the development of inferences. When you ask children to make inferences about a character's motivation, to explain how events from different parts of the story are connected, and compare and contrast characters or story events with their own experiences, you are providing opportunities for them to engage in analytical talk. To build vocabulary, you can point to parts of the illustration as you read particular words (such as pointing to the illustration of an acorn when you read about that object), dramatize (such as shaking with trepidation), or use your voice to emphasize meaning (such as using a silly voice to demonstrate a foolish character). Sometimes you can slip in a short phrase that defines a word as you read. Finally, when reading stories aloud, you will want to emphasize the problem of the story.

Transformed Instruction: Repeated Interactive Read-Alouds of Quality Literature

Based on this research, Dr. Judy Schickedanz and I (McGee & Schickedanz, 2007) developed an approach for reading aloud quality literature that we call Repeated Interactive Read-Alouds. This approach to reading books aloud is a systematic application of research and is grounded in our experiences reading aloud to many preschool children. To begin repeated interactive read-alouds, we select as core books several high-quality texts related to a topic or theme. These books will be read aloud several times during the unit of study and left in the book center for children to use after the read-aloud sessions. We select both storybooks and information books that feature these qualities:

- Content that will maximize children's understanding, engagement in analytical talk, and learning of new vocabulary words
- Storybooks with characters who have several character traits and problems that are somewhat familiar to young children
- Texts that provide many opportunities for children to grapple with meaning
- Information books that introduce new concepts using photographs and other illustrations
- Texts that provide clear explanations but also prompt children to analyze and reason

The lists on pages 61 and 62 present storybooks, nonfiction books, alphabet books, predictable books with patterned language, and books to elicit drama that are effective as core books for repeated interactive read-alouds for a Farm unit and a unit on Families and Friends.

In the sections that follow, I describe the repeated interactive read-aloud technique for using storybooks, and then describe how to modify the technique when reading aloud nonfiction informational books. I use many of the same techniques when reading information books as when reading storybooks but include some different techniques suited to the nature of informational text. The read-aloud activity includes three separate readings of the book. Table 3.1 shows lesson parts, teacher actions, and literary and literacy components for the first read-aloud of storybooks.

Table 3.1 Sample Activities for First Read-Aloud of *Farmer Duck*

Lesson Part	Teacher Actions/ Dialogue	Literary and Literacy Components
Book Introduction	*Pointing to the duck on the front cover and the field:* "This is a book about a farmer who is a duck. He lives with a farmer, but the farmer is so lazy he just stays in bed all day. This is a problem for Farmer Duck because he has to do all the farmer's work." *Pointing to the hoe at the end of this sentence:* "Here is Farmer Duck out in the field, and it looks like he's using a hoe to get the dirt ready to plant some seeds." *Displaying the front endpaper. Pointing to the barn and the farmhouse in the distance:* "Up here is where Farmer Duck lives." *Pointing to the trees:* "I'm thinking it is winter. There are no leaves on the trees."	*Cover Illustration* The cover illustration is used to draw children's attention to the main character as well as adding some information that could be inferred from the illustrations. An explicit statement identifies the main character and his situation—the duck in this book is a farmer—and that he will be doing lots of chores, such as working in the field. *Vocabulary* The word *hoe* is introduced and related to the object in the illustration. This simple technique is used to clarify the meaning of a word that may be new to children. *Book Parts* Several features of books can be used to help lead children into the story. These features include front- and back-cover illustrations,

Lesson Part	Teacher Actions/ Dialogue	Literary and Literacy Components
Book Introduction, *continued*	*Using the title page to highlight title, to convey an idea about the character and his situation, and to model a way of moving (trudging):* "The title of this book is *Farmer Duck*. He is trudging up to the farmhouse after a hard day of work."	frontispiece illustrations (illustrations before the title-page that may appear on the dedication page or page with ISBN information), the half and the full title page illustrations, and front and back endpapers. Note that some of these features may not be included in some books used for read-aloud in preschool. The term *title* is part of the literary vocabulary that children encounter as they participate in reading and writing activities.
Vocabulary-Enhancing Techniques	Techniques that focus children's attention on vocabulary that is important to the story line as well as other words that will extend their vocabulary: • facial expressions • dramatic motions • varied pacing • briefly interjecting to define a word or phrase • pointing to objects or actions in illustrations *Focusing attention on vocabulary in the text:* The duck *fetched* the cow from the field. *Pointing to the cow and the rope the duck is using to pull the cow:* "Look. Here is Farmer Duck fetching the cow out of the rain. He is pulling the cow into the warm barn."	*Terms in the text:* Words and phrases that are important to children's understanding of the characters and plot are identified while reading the story to the children. Many of these words are examples of literary language. The words selected should be sophisticated (beyond children's normal listening vocabulary), likely to be encountered in other settings (not so rare that children will never encounter them again), and important to the story line (Beck, McKeown, & Kucan, 2002). Words and phrases in the text of *Farmer Duck*: *lazy, fetched, fed up, upset, dawn, stole down the hall, creaked upstairs, waddled* *Terms not in the text:* This list includes words and phrases that are critical for understanding the story and represent language

continued . . .

Lesson Part	Teacher Actions/ Dialogue	Literary and Literacy Components
Vocabulary-Enhancing Techniques, *continued*		that teachers would likely use when talking about the story. Words and phrases not in the text: *hoe, miserable, share of the work, stand up for himself, not fair*
Comprehension-Enhancing Comments and Questions	Several techniques highlight selected story events and help sustain children's attention: • slowing down the reading • making eye contact with facial expressions reflecting how a character might feel at that point in the story • predicting what may happen next by using the phrase "I'm thinking . . ." to preface comments • looking away from the book while making "I'm thinking . . ." comments • following "I'm thinking . . ." comments with a question *Modeling inference:* Story event: The duck fetches the cow from the rain. "Poor duck and cow are out in the rain. That farmer is warm and dry up in his room [pointing to the farmer at the window]. I'm thinking that the cow feels wet and miserable. I bet she'll get dry in the barn." Questions and Answers (**T**eacher and **C**hildren): T: How do you think the cow is going to feel when she gets inside the barn? What will she be thinking?	*Story events:* Story events are identified and highlighted during reading to enable children to understand the story line: • events that introduce the problem to make sure children understand the chain of events leading up to the problem and its possible consequences • events in which the character attempts to solve the problem or when the problem gets even more complicated • event that indicates the story climax—usually occurs just prior to the end of the story and just prior to when the problem is solved Four events in *Farmer Duck* make effective places to stop and make comprehension-enhancing comments and questions: • Farmer Duck fetches the cow out of the rain and puts her into the barn. • The duck carries a sheep out in a snowstorm down the hill to the barn. • The duck puts the hens in their house.

Lesson Part	Teacher Actions/ Dialogue	Literary and Literacy Components
Comprehension-Enhancing Comments and Questions, *continued*	C: She will feel dry. T: Yes, she will now be dry. Will she be feeling miserable? When she is all dried out, what will she be thinking about the duck? C: She feels good. She feels happy. She likes the duck. T: Yes, she feels happy and relieved to be inside out of the rain. She is not miserable and wet, but comfortable and dry. She is grateful to the duck for helping her get inside. This pattern of questioning is repeated for other story events. The final event in *Farmer Duck* is when the cows, sheep, and hens hold a meeting about the situation with their friend the duck. The text says they were upset about the duck, they loved the duck, and they made a plan. T: I'm thinking the animals are upset because the duck is so tired all the time. The duck is so sad because he works and works, and the farmer just lays around. That is not fair. I'm wondering what their plan might be. What do you suppose the cows and sheep and hens are thinking about the farmer? C: That farmer is so lazy. It is not fair. He needs to work, too.	• The cows, sheep, and hens decide to do something so that Farmer Duck is not so sad. *Modeling comprehension behavior:* Comments and questions are used to scaffold children's understanding of story events and make inferences about how the characters think and feel. Consistent question patterns and elaboration of children's answers provide a model that children can rely on as they respond to other events in the story. Extended responses to children's answers provide models of thinking and talking that children observe and begin to use in their own responses. "I'm thinking . . ." is a signal that the teacher isn't reading the story, but is using her own ideas about the story and its characters. This pattern helps children make inferences. To answer questions about how the characters are feeling requires the children to use *analytical talk*. To understand the final event, children have to make inferences that are based on a number of conditions in the story. The "I'm thinking . . ." comment and follow-up question provide a model that children can use to continue the line of thinking.

continued . . .

Lesson Part	Teacher Actions/ Dialogue	Literary and Literacy Components
After-Reading Explanation Question	A final "after reading" question gives children an opportunity to connect ideas about previous events to the final event in the story. T: Why are the animals helping Farmer Duck? Cows and sheep and hens don't usually cut hay. That's not their job. Why are they helping the duck? Additional scaffolding questions and comments: • What do the animals think about the farmer? • What do the animals think about the duck? Did the animals think it was fair for the duck to do all the work by himself? • How are the animals going to make sure Farmer Duck doesn't have to do all the work himself now that the farmer is gone? I'm thinking those animals are really good friends to Farmer Duck. They want to help him do the work. It is only fair for everyone to do a little bit of work.	Illustrations at the end of the book provide a good backdrop for asking an explanation question. Additional questions based on the children's responses provide extra support that will help children elaborate on their ideas and form an explanation.

First Read-Aloud of Storybooks

First read-alouds have four major parts: book introduction, vocabulary-enhancing techniques, comprehension-extending comments and questions, and an after-reading question. The table on pages 64–68, based on the book *Farmer Duck* (Waddell, 1991), describes activities for each lesson part and explains literary and literacy components reflected in those activities.

Linda Rodgers reading Farmer Duck *in the book center*

An Interactive Read-Aloud and Shared Writing

Annie Walker and Katesha Washington have been exploring the theme
"Sens-a-tional Spring" during the month of April. As part of the theme, they
have learned about the five senses. Annie begins a discussion about the senses
before reading *My Five Senses* (Aliki, 1989). She invites children to identify
things they have seen, tasted, touched, heard, or smelled. As they respond, she
asks them to clarify and expand.

Andre:	I like to smell strawberries.
Annie:	I like to smell strawberries, too. They taste good too. They are pretty to look at.
Martha:	I like rain.
Annie:	What do you like about the rain? What senses do you use?
Martha:	Watching rain.
Annie:	You like to watch the rain and see it coming down.

Annie reads the title of the book and shows a page filled with many small
pictures of things children can see, hear, touch, smell, and taste. She says,
"These pictures are very small, and I know you can't see them. When I get
finished reading today, I am going to put the book back in the book center so
you can look through all these things you use your senses for." Then she reads
through the book and invites children to chime in, saying the repetitive phrases
in the text. She stops sometimes to point at and explain vocabulary words. She
points to the pine tree in the illustration and makes a vocabulary-enhancing
comment: "A pine tree is just like a Christmas tree. It stays green all year."

Annie stops on the page where the little boy in the story is playing with his puppy. She asks, "What senses is the little boy using when he laughs and plays with his puppy?"

Jamal: He feeling the puppy.

Annie: Yes, he is using his sense of touch to feel the puppy. What else?

Rob: He see the puppy.

Annie: Very good. He uses his eyes to see the puppy. What else?

Macy: Smell.

Annie: Yes, he could smell the puppy. I know another one.

Rose: Hear.

Annie: He could hear the puppy. Let's count how many senses we need to play with a puppy. *See, hear, smell,* and *feel*. We don't taste a puppy. We know we don't eat puppies so we can't use our taste.

After reading the book, Annie asks, "Why do we need our five senses?" For the first time during this read-aloud, all the children are silent. No one seems to understand the question. So Annie says, "What did the little boy do with the puppy?" Many children discuss seeing, hearing, smelling, and touching the puppy. Annie concludes, "The little boy is aware of the puppy. He can hear him and smell him and feel him and see him. If he didn't have eyes, what would happen?"

Martha: He be dead.

Annie: People without eyes don't die. They just can't see. So the little boy wouldn't be able to see the puppy. Our senses are important. We need them to see, and touch, and smell, and hear, and feel.

Katesha takes over for the next part of the lesson. She points to the shared-writing chart, on which she's written the title "The Boy Uses His Senses to . . ." She says to the children, "We are going to write a list today, telling what 'The Boy Uses His Senses to' do." As she reads, she points to each word in the title of the shared-writing chart. She asks, "Now what are some things the boy in the book uses his senses to do?" One child responds, "Dog," and Katesha says, "Yes, he did use his senses to touch a dog. Do you want to write *dog*?" The child steps up to the chart, and Katesha asks the group, "Dog. What sound does *dog* begin with?" A chorus of voices respond, "D," and Katesha says, "Yes, it begins with the letter *D*, but what sound does it begin with?" Now many children say /d/. Katesha's children are familiar with vowel sounds so she enunciates the short-*o* sound, and many children know that sound is spelled with the letter *O*. Next Katesha uses her sound/letter strategy to lead all children in listening to the ending sound /g/, say the sound, and then name the letter. The child sits down after spelling the word *dog* with the help of the children using the sound/letter spelling routine.

Now Katesha asks, "What did the little boy do with the dog? What was the sense he used?" Another child offers, "Touch," and the children are led through the spelling of that word, although Katesha must tell the child the spelling of *ou*. Katesha continues prompting the shared list by asking, "What else did the little boy use his senses for?" Eventually the children spell the words *touch*, *smell*, *hear*, and *see*. Katesha leads the children in rereading their shared-writing chart two times before children go off to their small-group tables.

Reinforcing Literacy: Second Read-Alouds

Second read-alouds are similar to first reads and should occur a day or two after first reads. They include the same four components and the same vocabulary is highlighted, although in slightly different ways. You may pose some of the same comprehension questions from the first read-aloud but also select additional events to use in the comment and question cycle. By using a different after-reading question, you provide an opportunity to extend children's story understanding even further. During first read-alouds, you are helping children make inferences about the main character's thoughts and feelings. In second read-alouds, you can have children consider what other characters are thinking or feeling.

Book Introduction

At the beginning of the second read, you can acknowledge that children are familiar with the story. For example, you might say, "This book is titled *Farmer Duck*, and we know he has a problem. Who remembers what his problem is?" Many children are likely to respond that the duck has to do all the work, while others may remember the farmer stayed in bed all day. To make sure that the children are clear about the problem, you might say, "Yes, the duck has to do the work because the farmer is lazy. He stays in bed and doesn't do any work. It isn't fair for the duck."

The second read is an occasion when you can draw children's attention to additional information about book parts, including illustrations on the cover, endpapers, frontispieces, or title pages. You may comment on how selected illustrations make you feel. For example, you might comment that the front endpaper in *Farmer Duck* makes you feel sad because it is so gray and dark.

Vocabulary Development

During second reads, you can continue to highlight the same vocabulary with one important difference. Now you can clarify more words by inserting short definitions as you read the text. Because children are more familiar with the story, you can pause to define words, but these definitions should still be slipped into the story reading so the text is read with little disruption.

Comprehension Development

Story events are highlighted in the second read-aloud, and you may ask some of the same questions that you used in the first reading but without making any comments. For example, after reading the page where the duck fetches the cow into the barn, you could ask, "How do you think the cow is going to feel when she gets inside the barn? What will she be thinking?" To encourage children to elaborate on their responses, you can use clarifying and extending comments similar to those used in the first read. Because the second reading provides new opportunities to extend children's comprehension, it is a good idea to select two or three new events about which you can make comments and ask questions. For example, for further comprehension work, you may select the two-page spread where the cow and sheep and hens are pushing the farmer out of his house and the illustration showing the animals telling the duck what they have done.

For the first illustration, you might comment, "I'm thinking the animals are really mad at the farmer. We know they are going to chase him down the road and off the farm. What do you think the animals are thinking right here in this picture?" Later, you could ask, "What do you think the farmer is thinking?" Comprehension-extending questions frequently draw children's attention to a character's thoughts and feelings, which must often be inferred. For the second illustration, you might comment, "I'm thinking the duck is really, really happy. Look, he jumped for joy and threw up his rake. What do you think the animals said to the duck? What are they saying?" You might follow up children's responses with a more probing question, such as "Why do you think the animals got rid of the farmer?"

Children highly engaged as their teacher reads aloud

After-Reading Questions

After-reading questions in both first and second reads serve the same purposes in developing children's oral comprehension: they call for extended explanation, analysis, and reasoning. For the second read of *Farmer Duck*, you might turn to the illustration of the farmer running off the farm for good and ask, "Do you think the animals were mean in running off the farmer?" Here, it is likely that children will provide "yes" or "no" answers. You can help children extend their answers by asking why they think that way.

Third Read-Alouds: Guided Reconstruction

Third read-alouds should occur a few days after the second read, when the story is still familiar but children will need to do some remembering across time. The purpose of the third read-aloud is to have children reconstruct the story rather than simply listen to it. I use the terms "guided reconstruction" and "guided recount" to describe this activity. In this activity, you invite the children to look carefully at each illustration in order to retell the story and to add explanations about what the characters are thinking and feeling. The additional explanations take the activity beyond mere retelling; children are giving an in-depth account of the story.

After center time, Linda Rodgers gathers her children on the carpet for guided reconstruction of *The Seven Chinese Sisters* (Tucker, 2003).

Linda:	What's the title of our book?
Children:	Seven Chinese Sisters.
Linda:	Yes, and do you know the problem?
Children:	(*overlapping*) That dragon. The baby. They had to get the baby.
Linda:	The dragon took the baby and wanted to eat her, but the other sisters came and got her back. Now what is happening here?
Children:	The sisters.
Linda:	What is different about the sisters?
Child:	They up and she little.
Child:	These standing up and baby sitting.
Linda:	The sisters are standing straight up but the baby can't stand up yet. The sisters are . . . ?
Children:	(*overlapping*) Big. Standing up.
Linda:	And the baby is . . . ?
Children:	Sitting down, little, a baby.

Teacher Reflection

Linda Rodgers reflects on guided reconstruction: "Guided reconstruction is a great way to see/hear if the children are understanding the story and to see if they can recall some of the plot of the story. Our class loves to do this activity, no matter what book. They like to tell me the story. They learn about characters, the beginning, middle, and ending of a story, as well as the problem or plot of the story. We discuss the problem and how we might fix it differently."

Linda and the children continue reconstructing the story. When they reach the page where the dragon is illustrated for the first time, Linda asks:

Linda:　What kind of dragon is he?

Children:　(*overlapping*) Red. Mean. Skinny. Hungry.

Linda:　He is very skinny because he is so hungry. What do you think he is thinking?

Children:　(*overlapping*) Get the baby. Noodle soup. He be hungry. He mean.

Linda:　I think he is thinking to himself, "I sure am hungry, and I smell something really good." How do you know the dragon smells something good?

Child:　That line there.

Linda:　Yes, that is the smell coming up from the noodle soup cooking.

Linda continues guiding the children into a complete reconstruction of the story. After the lesson, the children line up to go outside, chatting about karate, the baby, noodle soup, and mean dragons.

Book Introduction

At the beginning of the third read-aloud, you can ask children to tell the book's title and the story's problem: "Who remembers the title of this book?" "We all remember what Farmer Duck's problem is. Who wants to summarize what Farmer Duck's problem is for us?" Have two or three children explain the problem. You can then turn to other sections of the book (for example, the endpapers) and ask children to comment. Finally, you can turn to the title page and ask, "What is happening here?"

Vocabulary Development

You can continue to emphasize the same vocabulary during guided recounts and even ask children to remember particular words. For example, you might ask, "What sound did the stairs make as the big cow went up?" or "What is another word for *going to get?*" By using these kinds of questions, you can extend vocabulary meanings beyond the context of the story. Here is another example from *Farmer Duck*: You might comment that in the story the animals "stole up the stairs," but that doesn't mean they stole the stairs, it means they went very quietly because they weren't supposed to be there. As an example, you might mention that when you were little you used to steal into your sister's room. You didn't steal anything, but you weren't supposed to go in there so you had to "steal into" the room very quietly so no one would know. During this commentary, you could vary the level and tone of your voice to convey the notions of *quiet* and *secrecy*. You could then invite children to describe times when they sneaked into a place they weren't supposed to be.

Developing Comprehension

The question "What is happening here?" can be used frequently to prompt children to recount story events. Recounts include explanations for the actions that are not explicitly stated in the text. After prompting children to make extended recounts, you can read the text on the selected page. Depending on the length of the book, you may read some pages without inviting children to recount. During the third read-aloud, you may reread much of the book or allow children's recounts to stand for nearly all text while you reread only a few pages.

"What is going to happen next?" is another recount question you can ask when the following event is causally connected to the previous illustration. For example, one double-page spread in *Farmer Duck* shows the animals pushing the farmer out of the farmhouse and the following double spread shows them shooing him down a lane, over a hill, and off the farm forever. After reading the text under the first illustration, you can ask, "What is going to happen next?" because the second event is so connected to the current event in the illustration. This type of questioning encourages children to make predictions and enables them to recognize connections between story events. This activity helps children learn analytical talk.

After-Reading Questions

Guided recounts in third read-alouds end with yet another explanation question. For example, after reading *Farmer Duck* for the third time, you might ask, "Why do you think the duck didn't stand up for himself and just say, 'No. I'm not going to do all the work'?" To extend children's thinking even further, this is a good place for you to ask "what if" questions. For example, "What if the farmer had come back—what do you think the animals would do?" or "What if the animals hadn't run the farmer off, what do you think the duck might have done?" "What if" questions provide opportunities for children to draw on experience, make judgments about the "personalities" of story characters and how their behavior might change, and use imagination to expand on story events. As children contribute ideas in response to "what if" questions, you can scaffold children's conversations by inviting them to engage with the ideas offered by their classmates. "What do others think about that?" "Tell us what you are thinking" or "Tell us more so that we might understand, too" are examples of statements that you can use to facilitate a flow of conversation among the children.

Interactive Read-Alouds of Information Books

Ede Wortham has placed a new Big Book beside the easel and the children notice it almost immediately as they come into the classroom. The book is *Seeds Grow* (Walker, 1992) and is the book for the week. The children chat informally about the book before going on with some other activities.

Child: What's that?

Ede: That's our book for this week.

Child: Is that a balloon? [asking about the illustration of a seed with a small root and sprout on the book's cover]

Ede: Um, what do you think that could be?

Child: A hamburger?

Child: Shoe?

Child: Bug.

Ede: It is a very interesting-looking thing. It's not a hamburger or a balloon.

Child: What that thing? [pointing to roots]

Child: String?

Ede: Well, it is something that grows. It might be in our garden.

Child: A plant?

Ede: It is a plant and it is coming out of a seed. See here? And here are the roots and the leaves that are growing out of the seed casing.

Children: (*talking among themselves and overlapping*) Plant? That a plant? I don't see no plant. There go the leaves. Is that a seed? I don't see no seed. I'm going to do the flowers today.

When the children return from gym, they quickly sit on the carpet for the read-aloud. Ede introduces the book using the experiences from earlier in the morning: "When we first got here, we all looked at this strange picture and we had lots of ideas about what it could be. I have here a package that could help us think about this picture. What is in this package?"

Ede had taken a seed package from the second dramatic-play center, a flower shop, to show as a planned introduction to this read-aloud. Many children had shaken the package during center time, asked her about the contents of the package, and talked among themselves about the package. Ede had at least four conversations with different children about the seed packets during center time, so she knew interest was high about this new item in the classroom. To summarize the children's discussion about things that grow, Ede creates a web on chart paper. She will use this to keep track of the children's ideas.

When asked what was in the package, many children replied, "Seeds." Ede asked, "What do you do with seeds?" Many children responded: "Spread 'em out." "Plants will grow." "They be plants."

Now Ede draws attention back to the Big Book and, pointing to the illustration on the cover of the book, asks, "What is this?"

Many children respond that it is a seed, and Ede continues: "This morning when we first got here, we thought this was a strange picture. We thought this was a balloon, a hamburger, even a bug. But that's a seed. Is it a picture someone drew or a photograph?"

There are many ideas about whether it is a drawing that someone colored or a photograph. Finally, most children agree it is a photograph, and Ede asks, "What do we use to take a photograph?" Then she asks, "Who knew so many things can grow from a seed?" This opens a whole new set of questions from the children, who are still clearly puzzled about the cover illustration even after the earlier talk about seeds:

Child:　What that thing?

Child:　What that part?

Ede:　That is the seed casing and the seed comes up from the ground and the plant grows out of it. The straw-looking things are the roots.

Child:　I think, it dirt. They got dirt, I think it comed out of dirt.

Ede:　Yes, the seed grows out of the dirt and all plants come out of that.

Ede continues to read the book and discuss the illustrations. Then the children discuss other things that grow. Many children name plants they know: flowers, potatoes, carrots. Ede reminds the children these are all plants and she is wondering what else grows besides plants. She gives a hint by pointing to her teeth, saying, "Most of us have lost one of these and they grow." The children call out "Teeth," and Ede writes that on the web. Another child calls out "Animals," and Ede says, "Yes, animals grow, too" and writes that on the web. She continues to give hints by pointing to her hair and nails. She adds those ideas to the web until it is time for lunch.

Later, Ede notes, "The children had some interesting comments about the book of the week. The seed book discussion was one of those textbook 'teachable moments.' It was also a great reminder of just how literate 4-year-olds are. The illustration on the Big Book really did look like a hamburger or a bug."

In recent years, more attention has been focused on using information books in preschool programs. Today, quality information books are more widely available than in the past. It is critical to use nonfiction information books during repeated interactive read-alouds. This is especially critical because teachers seem to select more stories to share with young children, and most classroom libraries have fewer informational books than stories (Duke, 2000). You needn't worry that informational books will be uninteresting to children or too difficult. Research has demonstrated that reading informational books seems to spark extensive discussion (Pappas & Barry, 1997; Richgels, 2002; Smolkin & Donovan, 2002). Children spontaneously

Features of Informational Text

- Purpose is to inform, describe, or report
- Topics center on the natural and social world—animals, places, plants, people, environment, weather, etc.
- Organizational patterns include sequence, description, problem-solution, cause-effect, comparison-contrast
- Writing uses present verb tense (timeless verb)
- May include story elements (characters, setting, problem, resolution) with information embedded in the story
- Design and layout are used to differentiate story and factual details

ask questions about the information presented in these books. Children's natural curiosity arouses their interest even in books presenting technical information.

You have many options for how to present informational books in interactive read-alouds. You can read through these books as you would a storybook, or you can decide only to read certain portions of them. The decision to read all or a portion of an informational book will depend on the age and experiences of the children. However, repeated interactive read-alouds of information books always include reading the book (or portion of the book) three times.

The primary difference between repeated interactive read-alouds of information books compared to storybooks is the focus on physical causality (what causes events to occur) or natural sequences of events, such as cycles in nature, rather than on psychological causality (why characters act as they do). That is, problems in stories usually arise from characters who are motivated by some desire—this is psychological causality. Therefore, teachers frequently model making inferences about a character's feelings and thoughts when reading stories. In contrast, many informational books explain phenomena—why a hurricane is formed or how a snake captures and eats its prey. Embedded in such explanations are sequences of events sometimes linked by cause and effect relationships.

These events are related by physical causality or by sequences found in the natural world. When reading information books, teachers make explicit how the ideas in a text are linked together (Smolkin & Donovan, 2002) using words or phrases such as next, as a result, because, and that causes. As you read information texts, you can pause frequently to summarize events that have occurred so far, to link new information with information that has been previously read, and to connect new information to children's experiences.

Information books provide an especially rich context for discussing new vocabulary. As with storybooks, you can carefully select a few critical words or phrases to develop, the ones central to understanding the concepts presented in the book. During reading, you can use a phrase or short sentence to define a term and then reinforce the meaning of the technical word by saying, "this part of the text tells me what this word means. I'll read it again, and you listen to see if you can figure out what the word means."

Shared Reading

In shared reading, as the teacher reads aloud to children, the focus is not only on enjoying and understanding the book, but can also include attending to details of the printed text or to language patterns. Often teachers read from Big Books or enlarged charts so that all the children can see the printed text being read. However, shared reading does not require that you always use Big Books or enlarged charts. Sometimes you will read from regular-size books, especially when the focus is on language patterns. Other times, you may use Big Books in repeated interactive read-alouds when your focus is on developing vocabulary and oral comprehension. Thus, it is not the type of material that dictates whether teachers will use shared reading or repeated interactive read-aloud techniques (McGee & Morrow, 2005). Instead, the method of reading aloud is determined by the purpose for instruction. Table 3.2 shows the differences between shared reading and interactive read-aloud activities.

Because shared reading and interactive read-alouds have different instructional purposes, it is important not to mix the strategies when you read a single book. Rather, you need to be very clear about your purpose for reading a particular book aloud and deliberately use the most appropriate strategy for developing that purpose.

Table 3.2 Comparison of Shared Reading and Interactive Read-Alouds

Shared Reading Involves:	Interactive Read-Alouds Involve:
Children joining in "reading" by saying the text along with the teacher	Children listening as the teacher reads and answers questions when appropriate
Focusing children's attention on the printed text (of Big Books and charts) or on the language (rhyme, alliteration, or alphabet)	Focusing children's attention on vocabulary, elements in the illustrations, and comprehension of the ideas in the story or information book
Teaching concepts about print such as book orientation (top, bottom, front, back, page by page), directionality (left to right, return sweep, reading left page before right), and letter/word concepts (words are comprised of letters, words can be long or short, words are surrounded by spaces)	Focusing children's attention on how story characters think and feel
Introducing children to the language of print including the meanings of *word*, *letter*, *space*, *rhyme*, and *sentence*	Introducing children to the language used to describe stories including *characters*, *events*, *problems*, *solution to the problem*, *beginning*, *middle*, and *ending*

Research-Based Best Practices in Shared Reading

During shared reading, teachers point to the printed text as they read. Later, and more important, children attempt to point to print as they remember language patterns found in the text (Clay, 1998). Research has demonstrated that children learn to memorize shared texts easily, but have a more difficult time learning to point to words one by one (Ehri & Sweet, 1991). Most difficult, and usually not accomplished successfully until kindergarten, is the ability to point to each written word as a spoken word is recited, called finger-point reading. However, the process of learning to finger-point read helps children acquire concepts about print, especially directionality concepts and concepts about letters and words. They gradually learn that print is read word by word from left to right and line by line from top to bottom (Clay, 1998). Thus, the teacher's role is to systematically move from shared reading using Big Books or enlarged charts to finger-point reading using very short texts presented in pocket charts. In finger-point reading, it is important that the teacher control the length of text to ensure children can memorize the text. Spaces between words should be especially prominent so that children can more easily use spacing to guide finger-point reading.

> Shared reading, a special form of reading aloud to children, is especially beneficial for developing children's concepts about print (Clay, 1979).

Using Shared Reading to Develop Concepts About Print

Teaching children about features of print is a primary purpose of shared reading in preschool. As you read from enlarged texts, placed on an easel or hanging on a chart stand, the children are seated so that everyone can see the printed text. Books, poems, and texts used in shared reading are usually very easy to understand, and they frequently have a repeated pattern. Children naturally catch on to the pattern, and often spontaneously begin reading along with you. To help direct children's attention to the print, you can use a pointer to point to the words while reading. Big Books, commercially prepared charts of poems or songs, and teacher-made materials used in shared reading should have all these features (be careful—many commercial materials do *not* have these features):

- only one or two lines of text per page for Big Books
- fewer than eight lines of text for charts
- words printed in very large fonts
- large and prominent word spaces
- some repeated words
- short and easily remembered text

You may need to prepare your own shared reading charts so they have all the required features. Without them, children may not be able to distinguish individual words, necessary for developing concepts about print.

As you read from the enlarged print of a Big Book in shared reading activities, you can focus on developing book orientation concepts through explicit instruction. As you model appropriate ways to handle a book, you can point out the front and back of books and the top and bottom of pages, and how one reads the left page before the right page, and then turns to the

Concepts About Print That Can Be Taught During Shared Reading

Orientation of Books
- Front and back of the book
- Top and bottom of a page
- Title and title page
- Author and illustrator
- Dedication and dedication page

Directionality
- We read the left page before the right page
- After we read the right page, we turn to the next page
- We start reading at the first word in the line of text
- We read each word from left to right (left-to-right sweep)
- After we read a line of text, we sweep back to read the next line (return sweep)

Letter and Word Concepts
- Words are made up of letters
- Words have beginning and ending letters
- Words are long (they have many letters that can be counted)
- Words are short (they have just a few letters that can be counted)
- Words might be repeated
- Words can start with the same letter as other words
- Some words begin with a capital letter
- Words are separated by spaces
- Words can be substituted to make a new text

next page. You can demonstrate how to open the book to the title page and then to locate the first page of the story. You can also target directionality concepts. For example, you could say, "Let me point out exactly where I am going to start reading. Put your eyes right up here. Now I am going to read across the line like this." Here, you are making it explicit that you will begin reading at the left on the top line of print, read across that line, and return to the left on the next line of print. After children have had many opportunities to observe your demonstrations, you can ask them to show where you should begin to read and where your eyes should move as you read the page.

A list of concepts about print that you can help children develop through shared-reading activities is provided on page 81. Shared reading is most effective when you select only one or two concepts to teach as you read a book or chart. You can continue to focus on these few concepts as you read one or two books or charts, until children demonstrate an awareness of those concepts. Then you can select other concepts for attention.

Later, as children gain book orientation and directionality concepts, you can focus on demonstrating more complex concepts about words and letters.

Finger-Point Reading

In finger-point reading children point to written words while reciting them aloud. Finger-point reading is a technique you can use to develop more advanced concepts about print. In this activity, you are providing explicit instruction about letters and words, including awareness of the spaces used to separate words. Pocket charts are the most manageable materials to use for this activity.

You will need to prepare shorter texts that children can easily memorize. These texts consist of a meaningful sentence or two (15 to 20 words) from a familiar song, poem, or story on sentence strips or word cards. The first (and where needed, second) sentence of a story or poem is usually a good selection for pocket chart shared-reading activities. For example, you may select the text "Brown bear, brown bear/what do you see?/I see a green frog/looking at me." from the book *Brown Bear, Brown Bear, What Do You See?* for a four-line text presented on a pocket chart. The words would be printed on four sentence strips using larger than normal word spaces. You model reading the pocket chart text several times, using a pointer to point under each word as you read. Children are invited to join in and read the sentence as you point. Then individual children are given opportunities to point to the words as other children repeat the sentence (usually you will need to guide children to point to the correct word as the sentence is spoken). You can demonstrate, and then invite children to perform other activities to develop concepts about words and letters. For example, children can use their hands to isolate just one word on the pocket chart, to match words printed on index cards with words

Finger-Point Reading Instruction

To teach children the text, teachers:

- Read and reread the text many times as children echo
- Use choral reading techniques as children chime in
- Read loudly and softly
- Read in a kitty voice, a man's deep voice, a silly girl's voice
- Have different children read different lines of text (use different colors of markers to print each line of text)
- Anticipate what will be read before actually reading it (stop reading before a line of text and ask children to say what the line of text will say)

To teach children to use finger-point reading to locate and identify words, teachers:

- Demonstrate finger-point reading
- Have children use very short pointers or their finger to point to each word
- Demonstrate holding finger in place for longer words (teach two- and three-beat words—words for which you have to hold your finger still for two or three beats)
- Demonstrate using finger-point reading to identify a word (turn the word in the pocket chart over so that there is a blank space for the word; say "I'm going to use my finger to figure out this word," then demonstrate starting at the beginning of the line, finger-point reading and stopping at the word, then saying it)
- Have children use finger-point reading to identify words (teach children to start either at the beginning of the whole text or at the beginning of a line of text and track to identify the word)
- Demonstrate how to locate a word (say, "I want to find the word *looking* and I can use finger-point reading to find it by reading and pointing until I hear the word, and then I stop;" demonstrate starting at the beginning of the text, finger-point reading, and stopping at the word *looking*)

written on the pocket chart, or to find long and short words. The chart on page 83 summarizes finger-point reading instruction.

Using Shared Reading to Develop Language-Pattern Concepts

Shared reading can also be used to draw children's attention to patterns in language, such as the alphabet, rhyming words, or alliteration. Alphabet books make excellent books to use in shared reading. Big Book versions of favorite alphabet books are available, and the most appropriate versions are those with little text per page. If possible, you should have three or four big alphabet books in the classroom. At the end of reading a page, you may pause to develop some language pattern concepts. With alphabet books, you may ask children to remember words they read on that page that begin with a specific letter, for example, the letter *B*. You can remind children that all the words that begin with the letter *B* have the same beginning sound.

There are many excellent books that have numerous rhyming words, and many of these are also available in Big Book format. Poems are excellent sources of rhyming words, and you can create your own charts of favorite poems. After reading a page or line of rhyming text, you can invite children to remember two words that rhyme. Although not as plentiful as rhyming books and poems, you can find poems and books that feature alliteration. These texts can be read in the same way as those with rhyme. With these texts, you can draw children's attention to the repeated patterns and invite children to play with those patterns by making up a new sentence using the language pattern. You'll want to make children aware of other types of patterns as well, such as repeated words and phrases. For example, one teacher helped a group of 3-year-olds use the pattern of *Brown Bear, Brown Bear* to make up a Halloween poem: "Orange pumpkin, orange pumpkin, what do you see? I see a white ghost looking at me."

Reading with a focus on the same concept enables children to grasp the concept more quickly. I have found that it is more effective for teachers to draw attention only to patterns in language or to concepts about print rather than drawing children's attention to both in the same book.

The Value of Drama and Retelling

Drama and retelling activities are especially helpful in expanding children's comprehension and vocabulary (McGee, 2003). The most effective use of drama and retelling for literacy development is dramatizing a folktale that includes just a few characters and repeated dialogue. Dramatizing folktales with these characteristics is easier for young children when several children act out the part of each character. In this way, a group of children, rather than one individual child, remembers the dialogue. Furthermore, this activity provides opportunities for all children, including those who are shy or are learning English, to participate.

Research-Based Best Practices in Drama and Retelling

Ample research suggests that retelling and dramatizing stories increase children's language and literacy concepts. Research findings have indicated the following:

- Preschoolers and kindergartners who frequently act out stories that have been read aloud to them have better vocabularies, use more complex syntax, and have better story comprehension than children who draw or talk about stories (Pellegrini & Galda, 1982; Saltz & Johnson, 1974).

- When teachers guide story dramatizations by providing suggestions for how children can act, model creating dialogue, or take a role in drama, children's learning increases (Pellegrini & Galda, 1990; Williamson & Silvern, 1991).

- Further, more children engage in drama when teachers reread stories frequently and demonstrate when and how to use props (Martinez, Cheney, & Teale, 1991).

- Five-year-olds who repeatedly listen to and then retell informational books recall more information and use the particular features of language found in informational books (Pappas & Brown, 1988; Pappas, 1991; 1993).

- Repeated retelling of storybooks with teacher guidance and feedback also facilitates children's comprehension and the quality of language they recall (Morrow, 1984; 1988; Morrow & Smith, 1990).

Transformed Practices: Whole-Group Drama

The first step in whole-group drama is to present the target book to be dramatized so that children fully explore its meaning. I have found that complex folktales provide highly effective prompts for creating drama. For example, *The Three Billy Goats Gruff* (Stevens, 1995) includes both repeated dialogue and many places in the text where children can draw inferences about character motivation (e.g., why does the little goat dress as a baby and what is the result of that action? Why does the second billy goat dress up in pants that are so large and what is the result of that action?). Thus, the book is worthy of being used in whole-group drama.

Once children are familiar with the book and its dialogue, you introduce the drama activity. Each child is given a prop to represent the character he/she will portray. I have found a simple drawing of an animal's or character's face is

Children using drama props

sufficient. Drama props may include a picture strung on a necklace or a puppet taped to a straw or wooden stick. The prop identifies the character that the children will enact.

I recommend that drama take place while children are sitting or standing in the whole-group circle. It is easier to manage the drama if children sit or stand next to all the other children who are acting out the same part. Similarly, it is easier to manage the activity if you assign children parts rather than allow them to select which part they will play. You can remind children that the props will be in the book center later, and they can select any part they want during center play time. You perform the role of the narrator and guide children to create dialogue for their characters. For example, to narrate *The Three Billy Goats Gruff*, you may say, "This is the story *The Three Billy Goats Gruff*. Three billy goats live on one side of a valley and they have eaten all the grass. They want to cross the river to eat the sweet green grass on the other side. But to get to the sweet green grass, they must cross a bridge. A mean, ugly troll lives under the bridge. One day, the billy goats made a plan to cross the bridge." Then you would remind the children of the first character: the little billy goat. You would guide children in making the sound of his hooves on the bridge ("trip trap, trip trap") and then guide the troll to deliver his famous response: "Who's that tramping over my bridge?" Often children will say different words as they try out the dialogue of different characters— this is fine. You continue guiding the drama, prompting children when to speak and saying each character's dialogue along with the children. After dramatizing the story, you can put a copy of the book and story props in the book center for children's independent dramatization.

The next day or a few days later, you can reintroduce the drama by passing out the drama props again, making sure children have different parts than

Recommended Stories for Drama and Retelling

Three Little Kittens by Paul Galdone

Fiddle-I-Fee by Melissa Sweet

The Enormous Carrot by Vladimir Vagin

The Enormous Potato retold by Aubrey Davis

The Enormous Turnip by Kathy Parkinson

The Gingerbread Boy by Paul Galdone

The Pancake Boy by Lorinda Bryan Cauley

The Runaway Tortilla by Eric Kimmel

Goldilocks and the Three Bears by Bernadette Watts

Goldilocks and the Three Bears retold by Jan Brett

Deep in the Forest by Brinton Turkle

Henny Penny by Paul Galdone

Henny Penny by H. Werner Zimmerman

The Story of Chicken Licken by Jan Ormerod

I Know an Old Lady Who Swallowed a Fly by Nadine Bernard Westcott

I Know an Old Lady Who Swallowed a Pie by Alison Jackson

There Was an Old Lady Who Swallowed a Fly by Simms Taback

There Was an Old Lady Who Swallowed a Trout! by Teri Sloat

The Little Red Hen by Paul Galdone

The Little Red Hen by Lucinda McQueen

The Little Red Hen (Makes a Pizza) retold by Philemon Sturges

Cook-a-Doodle-Doo! by Janet Stevens and Susan Stevens Crummel

The Old Man's Mitten retold by Yevonne Pollock

The Mitten adapted by Jan Brett

The Mitten by Alvin Tresselt

The Woodcutter's Mitten by Loek Koopmans

The Three Billy Goats Gruff by Paul Galdone

The Three Billy Goats Gruff retold by Janet Stevens

Three Cool Kids by Rebecca Emberley

The Three Little Pigs by Gavin Bishop

The Three Little Pigs by Paul Galdone

The Three Little Pigs by James Marshall

Wiley and the Hairy Man by Molly Garrett Bang

Wiley and the Hairy Man retold by Judy Sierra

Little Red Riding Hood by John Goodall

Little Red Riding Hood by James Marshall

Little Red Riding Hood by Trina Schart Hyuman

those they had for the previous dramatization. During this second dramatiza-tion, you can continue to guide the children but provide less support than in the first dramatization. Now as children reenact the story, their drama becomes more elaborate and their language is expanded. Several days later, you can have the children dramatize the story again. By this time, children have practiced saying three different characters' dialogue.

Transformed Practices: Small-Group Retelling

Dramatizing stories in a whole group paves the way for a more difficult activity for preschoolers: retelling an entire story. Because of its complexity, retelling is only appropriate for small groups. To prepare for retelling, you should select one of the stories that has already been dramatized and create a set of very simple props for each child. For example, small pictures of the heads of the three billy goats and the troll can be reproduced, cut, and placed in small envelopes. There should be enough sets of props for each child in the small group. As in whole-group drama, you guide the children in using their props to retell the entire story. First, you model retelling a short part of the story and then invite children to retell that part. Next, you model retelling the second part of the story and children practice. You can repeat this cycle of teacher modeling and children practicing, scene by scene, until the story is finished. By this time, children should be sufficiently familiar with the story that they can practice retelling it to a partner. As you observe the children's retellings, you can praise them for their creative use of words and improvisations. After several retellings, you can encourage children to make up new scenes or even a new story to tell. A recommended list of folktales to use in dramatization and retelling activities in preschool is provided on page 87.

Summary

Embedded, purposeful language and literacy instruction transforms read-alouds and dramatizing activities by providing opportunities for children to contribute and participate in ways that are personally meaningful. As you focus children's attention on story characters and events, they become aware of ways that reading can lead to enjoyment and learning. Repeated interactive read-alouds are used to develop carefully selected vocabulary and high-level comprehension strategies. Shared reading and finger-point reading are used to develop concepts about print and language patterns. Drama and retelling are used to extend children's use of literary and decontextualized language, their ability to sustain participation in extended-language events, and their comprehension of favorite folktales. Your systematic use of embedded instruction maximizes opportunities for you to provide explicit instruction that focuses on helping children acquire concepts that will facilitate their later literacy development.

CHAPTER 4

Transforming Writing With Young Children

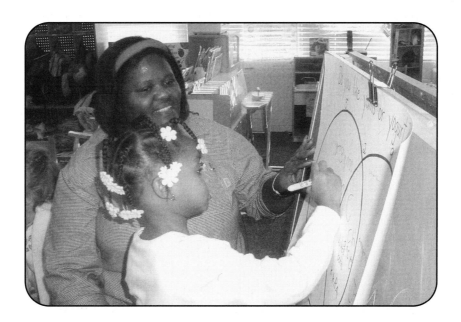

Ede Wortham, a pre-kindergarten teacher you have met in previous chapters, makes writing an integral part of children's activities in centers and through small-group guided instruction. During center time, she passes through the room and reminds children throughout to place any writing they wish to share on her rocking chair. When center time is over and the children are seated on the carpet, Ede takes all the papers that children

Ede's rocking chair with children's writing on it

have left on her chair. The transcript below shows the interactions between Ede and the children about their writing.

Ede: *(taking the children's papers)* Let's see what people wrote about today. Saphria, tell us about your writing.

Saphria: I wrote first my mama dead. Then I wrote I sleeping.

Ede: Your mama is dead? No. No. That isn't right. She is sleeping just like you. Good job. Patrick, tell us about your writing.

Patrick: I wrote "crab" up there, and over there "shark," and up there "alligator." Then I wrote "blue water." *(Patrick was earlier included in a small group that discussed animals they would see at the Sea Lab, and he has drawn pictures of his favorite animals.)*

Ede accepts Patrick's statement that he *wrote* even when it is clear he was drawing pictures. Then she draws attention to Patrick's signature that he has written on the paper vertically rather than horizontally.

Ede: You did some very interesting writing right here. Everyone look. Usually we write our name this way at the top *(gesturing left to right)*, but Patrick wrote his name down this way. Look he's got all his letters in his name. Good job. Kecia, tell us about your writing.

Kecia: I wrote numbers.

Ede: Yes, you did, and why did you write numbers? *(Ede had observed Kecia writing in the flower shop during center time.)*

Kecia: I, I, the flowers, I, flowers are free.

Ede: Oh, you were writing numbers for the price of the flowers. I had to pay forty-five dollars for a bouquet the other day. I thought that was pretty expensive. Myles did some kid writing today. Myles, tell us about your kid writing.

Myles: I drew all the team and then I wrote "team."

Ede: Yes, you did. Everyone look at this. Myles listened to "team" and heard *T M* and he wrote it right here. That was fabulous. Now it's time for gym, and we are going to listen to the sounds at the end of our names.

The children line up, listening to the sounds at the end of their names, and Ede moves around near them, making eye contact so they will know when to line up. At the same time, she is able to observe how readily children recognize the final sound in their names.

something I knew

Writing activities in Ede's classroom are helping children acquire many understandings about writing, such as using personal experience to select a topic, communicating something of personal interest, and using knowledge of letter-sound relationships. In brief, they are learning about purposes for writing and are applying strategies they have acquired in other lessons. These experiences are fostering in the children a sense of confidence as writers.

Writing Development in Preschool

Writing provides an example of one of the most interesting transformations in preschool language and literacy instruction. At one time, writing was not a focus of preschool. Of course, children were encouraged to draw and talk about their products; however, little if any attention was given to explicit instruction that enabled them to acquire foundational skills for writing. Today, there is growing acceptance of writing as a critical part of children's preschool experiences. This recognition has resulted in more effective methods for accelerating preschool children's writing development and produced a systematic approach to supporting and extending children's writing. This approach involves getting the classroom ready, initiating whole-group routines that demonstrate writing, using small-group activities to provide guided practice in writing, and establishing daily routines to celebrate and recognize children's writing accomplishments.

The Development of Early Writing

In general, most children's writing follows a similar pattern of development. Children in preschool may exhibit many behaviors that represent different points in writing development: scribbling and representational drawing, forming mock letters and other symbols, forming words, and invented spelling. At first, when toddlers begin to hold crayons, markers, and pencils, their marks on paper are uncontrolled scribbles. At this phase of writing, most children do not differentiate writing and drawing. Later, children learn to control arms, hands, and fingers so they can make lines, dots, and circles—the building blocks of all drawing and writing (Gardner, 1980). Around three years of age, children also begin to make representational drawings; these are usually drawings of people that have elements that look like people. Children make a circle for the head, lines for legs and arms, and dots for facial features. These symbolic drawings represent a critical shift in children's thinking that is reflected in their play as well as drawing. Now children can "pretend" to be a bear and gather little rocks as "berries" to eat. The little rocks are symbols that stand for "berries," just as the circle, lines, and dots in their drawings are symbols that stand for "people."

As children develop the ability to create representational drawings, they often notice the print in their environments and begin to pretend to write. At first, their early writing looks like scribbles, often consisting of nothing but up and down marks or little scratches. Some children make more controlled lines of scribbles that look like mock cursive writing rather than randomly placed scribble scratches. Figure 4.1 presents an example of scribble scratches written on a "prescription pad" in the doctor dramatic-play center, and 4.2 presents a more controlled linear scribble written at a writing center.

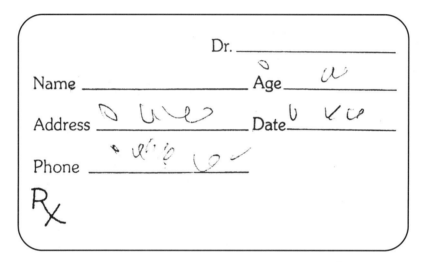

Figure 4.1 *An example of scribble scratches written on a "prescription pad"*

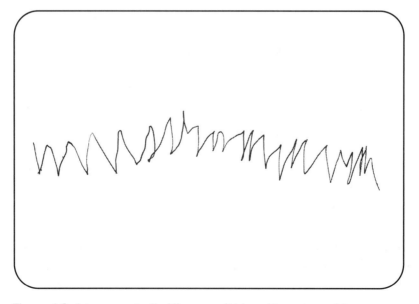

Figure 4.2 *A more controlled linear scribble written at a writing center*

Supporting Children in the Scribble Phase

Centers that are stocked with writing materials are places where children can experiment with writing using a variety of tools. For example, you can use drawing activities in the art center to encourage children in the phase of scribble writing. These activities can include clear demonstrations of drawing large and small circles, writing lines of many lengths and orientations, and placing dots around the page with different-colored crayons. The writing center is the obvious place for focusing children's attention on various specifics of writing. You can join the children here and participate by pretending to write using circles, lines, and dots. Because children usually choose to imitate their teacher, modeling shows them how to use more control as they form shapes that they will eventually transform into letters. These shared activities, including talk about writing, are effective ways to encourage children to express themselves in writing and to learn the building blocks for all drawing and writing—how to make controlled lines, circles, and dots. Although you may be tempted to model how to write letters while working with children in the writing center, there are other times that are more appropriate for this activity.

> When children pretend to write a message, we say they have developed the "sign concept"—awareness that all printed messages carry meaning (Clay, 1975).

Inviting children to share their writing acknowledges that you and others are interested in what they have to say. Recall how Ede Wortham set the stage for children to participate by inviting them to "tell us about your writing." Rather than asking children what their writing says, this more open-ended invitation allows children to make up a message or to describe what they are doing with their marks.

ask children

Even young children can learn that writing is done for a purpose, and it is easy to demonstrate this concept when you write with children. For example, you might say, "I'm going to write a list of things I'm going to buy at the grocery store." Some children in the scribble phase of writing may also pretend to write a message (e.g., "I wrote 'I love you'").

Supporting Children in the Symbol Salad Phase

Two aspects of writing may emerge near the end of the scribble phase: children's control over writing marks that approach conventional shapes, including circles, lines, and dots; and children's awareness that writers intentionally write to convey a message.

Children's use of letter-like shapes, called "mock letters," and other symbols marks the beginning of a new phase in their writing development. Their writing now includes a series of individual shapes rather than a line of scribbles. At first, the shapes do not have many features of real letters, but

Figure 4.3 *An example of "symbol salad" written as a grocery list in the grocery store dramatic-play center*

Shopping List

Figure 4.4 *A grocery list produced in the grocery store dramatic-play center*

eventually most children experiment with making up letter-like shapes. Writing with letter-like shapes and symbols is sometimes called "symbol salad" (McGee & Richgels, 2003). Figure 4.3 presents an example of symbol salad written as a grocery list in the grocery store dramatic-play center. The child who wrote this sample, when asked to talk about his writing, said, "I just wrote." Notice that the writing has separate symbols and most do not yet resemble letter-like forms, but rather look more like little drawings.

Children in the symbol salad phase of writing are ready for explicit instruction about writing letters. This instruction, though focused on the mechanics of writing, should still be purposeful and meaningful. For example, you might say, "I'm going to write a birthday card today to my mother. I'm going to write lots of E's and M's. E for *Evalee* and M for *Mom*. What letters are you writing?" Prominent displays of the ABC's in the writing center provide resources that you can refer to as you model writing. Children can find letters on the charts and refer to them for help when writing on their own. As you talk about letters and help children learn to identify letters, you will see that their writing includes more letter-like shapes. These mock letters include many features of conventional letters so that they look almost like real letters. Figure 4.4 presents a grocery list produced in the grocery store dramatic-play center that includes several mock letters and letters that are approaching conventional.

Moving on to Conventional Letters

Children eventually write mostly conventional letters, although orientation difficulties can be expected. At this next phase of writing, in addition to having more conventionally written letters, children shift from focusing on letters to showing interest in words. They write strings of letters with spaces that indicate words, and they enjoy copying words from familiar text. These behaviors indicate that children are ready for additional instruction in writing. At this stage, children probably know several words that they have encountered in shared reading and writing activities and want to copy some of these words in their writing. Demonstrating how to find words they know enables children to include these words when they write a message. For example, you might say, "I'm going to write 'I Like Me.' But first, I'll look at the book *I Like Me*. I like that book a lot. Let me go get it so I can use it to help me with my writing."

Children in the letter and word phase of writing make effective use of carefully selected word cards placed in the writing center. These may include a ring of index cards with children's photographs and names or rings of themed words, such as the line drawings and names of farm animals. Children make effective use of a set of words for writing Mother's Day cards, grocery lists, or even license plates. At this phase, children are interested in copying meaningful words rather than learning to spell. However, because they are centering attention on words that are important to them, they are incidentally developing awareness about how letters are put together to form words.

The Emergence of Invented Spelling

Finally, children begin to spell words on their own using a process called invented spellings (Richgels, 2001). Children may listen for the beginning sound and write a letter to represent that sound. At the beginning of trying to invent spellings, children often add a string of unrelated letters to fill out their word. Later, children learn to hear and spell two or more sounds in words. Figure 4.5 presents an example of an invented spelling of the word *play*. The child said the word slowly, listening to the first sound, /p/, and repeating it three times. He said, "P," and wrote a letter that looked like a *D* (probably intending this to be a *P*). He said the word slowly again and then added the letter A. Thus, he invented a spelling for this word that captured two of its sounds with a reasonable sound-to-letter match.

Children in the invented spelling phase of writing development can benefit from charts of letter-sound relationships (a chart of the consonant letters each with a picture to prompt recall of letter-sound relationships). As in other writing activities, talking with children acknowledges their writing, can help extend their invented spelling, and encourages them to expand on their message. For example, you might say, "I see you wrote 'play.' What do you like to play?"

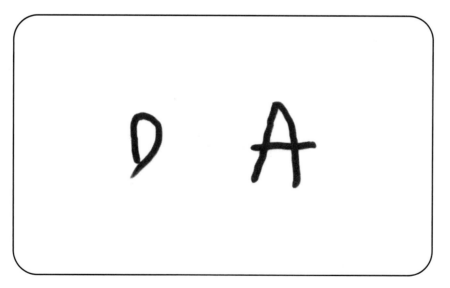

Figure 4.5 *An example of an invented spelling of the word* play

Getting the Classroom Ready

Children need an environment that shows various forms of writing and conveys a clear message about the role of writing in everyday activities. Consequently, the writing center is a critical area in the classroom where children can observe writing being modeled and talk about their writing. (See Chapter 2 for a description of a well-stocked writing center.) However, children can take advantage of opportunities for writing activities in other centers. Recall that one of the children in Ede Wortham's class wrote about something she was interested in from playing in the flower shop dramatic-play center. This is an example of a child's authentic use of writing during play. Similarly, the child who wrote the prescription (Figure 4.1) and the child who wrote the shopping list (Figure 4.3) were using writing props and materials available in different centers. These children had incentives to engage in purposeful and meaningful writing.

The Role of the Writing Center

Children will soon recognize that the writing center is the place where they can write and talk about their writing. The center needs to be large enough for at least two children and the teacher to sit comfortably with materials close at hand. Displays of writing samples, including shared-writing charts and models of writing, provide resources that children can refer to as they write and that you can use when interacting with children in the center.

The writing center provides the setting for conversations with children about how to go about writing and the ideas they have expressed in their writing. These conversations, intended to model writing for a purpose, help children accomplish what they are attempting to do. Children are supported in deciding what to write, selecting materials, and talking about their writing. Talking with children about their writing provides opportunities to ask questions to further their concepts. For example, you might ask, "Are you writing a list or a message?" or "Who are you writing the message to?" or "How will you send your message?" Sometimes children will decline to answer or simply say, "I'm just writing," which is perfectly fine. They're writing, and that's what counts.

Because activities in the writing center are focused on purposes for writing, correcting children's writing and insisting on standard letter formation at this time is neither necessary nor appropriate. However, as you engage in the kind of writing that children are using, you may occasionally demonstrate using more conventional writing. These incidental experiences contribute to other explicit experiences that support children's movement into another phase of development.

Adding Reading and Writing Materials

Research into literacy-rich homes has shown that children's experiences with reading and writing are embedded in their everyday life experiences. Children see parents writing checks, so they pretend to write checks; they see parents writing and reading grocery lists, so they write and pretend to read grocery lists. Recall from Chapter 2 descriptions of familiar settings with authentic objects that prompt children to pretend to read and write in ways they have observed their parents and others do in their homes and communities. Therefore, children are more likely to pretend to read and write in the home-living center when it is supplied with familiar props such as notepads, calendars, telephone message forms, greeting cards, address labels, menus, posters, and so on. Similarly, appropriate writing props, representative of items used in various roles, can be included in other centers and modified to fit with changes in center themes.

Modeling Use of Materials in Play

Modeling how to use writing materials in their play helps children to expand their ideas about purposes and forms of writing. In these activities, children are introduced to various roles and kinds of writing that people in those roles might do. For example, the book *Building a House* (Barton, 1990) provides the focus for modeling use of writing materials in the block center. Modeling how to draw a blueprint of a new house or how to order lumber for the house supports children in using new forms of writing for different purposes.

Writing telephone messages, a popular form of pretend writing in many preschools, can take place in any center. Because children are usually familiar with verbal telephone messages, modeling written messages helps them become aware of other ways to convey information received by telephone. Figure 4.6 presents an example of a teacher's phone message and a child's phone message.

Merely stopping in a center for a minute or two to model reading or writing is not likely sufficient to enrich children's play. A recent experience I had in a preschool classroom illustrates how clearly defined modeling can extend children's language and play scripts.

Several children were playing in a bakery. One child approached me with a paper and pencil and said, "Your number?" I was not sure what she was doing until another child said, "You say your phone number." So I did, and the children wrote a series of symbols including some mock letters and some numbers. Then another child approached and said, "What would you like today?" Soon the first child approached again and said, "Your number?" She wrote the "numbers" and asked me four more times, each time writing numbers and symbols. The teacher observed this and came over to me, saying, "I guess tomorrow we are going to use whole-group time to model more about this bakery. I'm not sure what to do to get children to extend their play beyond repeatedly asking a single question."

Together, the teacher and I brainstormed several roles played in the bakery, including a customer, a counter clerk, a baker, and a delivery person. We thought of all the reasons for going to a bakery and what could be purchased. We thought of all the texts that might be read and written, including maps (for delivery persons), recipes, order forms, receipts, checks, and credit card receipts. As a result of our collaboration, this richer conceptualization helped the teacher work with her children during a few minutes of whole group for the following two weeks. After this experience, the difference in the amount and variety of language children produced playing in that center was dramatically transformed.

Figure 4.6 *An example of a teacher's phone message and a child's phone message*

Teaching Children to Write With a Purpose

Children who live in literacy-rich homes see their parents and others read and write for a variety of purposes. Unfortunately, not all children have these experiences. Therefore, these children need frequent opportunities in school to interact with printed texts in ways that people do in everyday activities. Children must see reading and writing as meaningful to their lives if they are later to acquire the skills associated with conventional reading and writing (Duke & Purcell-Gates, 2003). Sign-in and other name-writing activities and shared writing are practices that show children different kinds of texts and different functions served by texts. Because children's signatures are important and meaningful to them, activities using their names are critical for 3-year-olds and early in the year for 4-year-olds.

Name-Writing Activities

Names are the first words to which children attend, and most children learn to recognize their names before they learn to identify any alphabet letters (Bloodgood, 1999). Therefore, children's names provide an immediate resource to teach a variety of early literacy concepts. The sign-in procedure (Harste, Burke, & Woodward, 1983) is one name-writing activity that can be used throughout the school year. Children write their names on special sign-in sheets as they enter the classroom. These sheets serve as attendance records for teachers and, when collected systematically, can be used to assess children's writing development. With 3-year-olds, the procedure may simply be to place their name card on a chart as they enter the classroom. Later they can find their name card and write their name on a small specially cut paper and put it in an attendance box (McGee & Richgels, 2003). Four-year-olds can sign in on colored attendance sheets placed on clipboards in specific locations around the room. Each sheet would be sectioned and include a model of each child's name. Up to four children may be included on one sign-in sheet and each sheet would be copied on different-colored paper and placed in a special location in the classroom. As children enter the classroom, they locate their sign-in sheet and use the model of the name to copy their name. Figure 4.7 presents a sign-in sheet typical for 4-year-olds mid-year.

Naturally, most 4-year-olds' signatures will not be conventional at the beginning of the year. What is important is that children remember their clipboard location, have a strategy for identifying which name is theirs on the sign-in sheet, and are willing to attempt to write their name. As children gain practice writing letters and develop more motor control, their signatures will become more conventional.

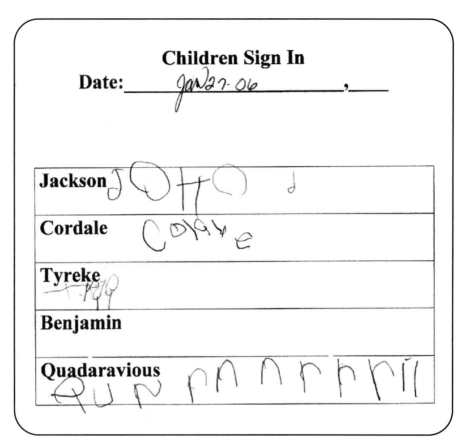

Figure 4.7 *A sign-in sheet typical for 4-year-olds mid-year*

Writing both first and last names is a big step for 4-year-olds and not all of them are ready for this task. At the outset, when children attempt to write both names, their writing seems to regress. With additional time and practice, children's writing begins to take on more conventional appearance as children control the size of their writing to accomplish the longer and more complex task of writing a first name and last name separated by a space.

The sign-in procedure can be varied in several ways to ensure that children's interest is sustained. For example, different kinds of pens can be provided, a name writer of the day can be selected to be a line leader, stickers can be placed on children's signatures that are deserving of recognition, or children's names can be moved to a new group of names.

The "name game" (adapted from Cunningham & Allington, 2007) is another writing activity that I recommend. In the name game, children are taught to recognize and write the name of one of their classmates. They practice matching alphabet letters to the name and may practice writing that name, depending on the age and experience of the children. This activity is best used with 4-year-olds, and the preparation is quite simple. At the beginning of the year, each child is given a sheet of paper with another child's name printed (in upper- and lowercase letters) at the top of the page and an envelope with cut-out letters that spell the name. With teacher guidance, the children select each alphabet letter, name it, and match it with the letters in the name. Children can draw a picture of the child and may glue the letters onto the paper to spell the name. The child whose name is being practiced gets all the pages stapled together to take home. This activity is most effective in a small group, where each child in the group has a day on which his or her name is featured. This lesson is effective for 3-year-olds later in the year. For 4-year-olds, the name game can become even more complex later in the year. Children can practice writing each classmate's name with teacher guidance.

Three-year-olds enjoy many activities using their names and the names of their classmates. A sentence strip puzzle is one activity that 3-year-olds can manage and enjoy. The puzzle consists of a child's picture pasted on the sentence strip with both a typed and printed version of his or her name. The strip is cut into three pieces using a jigsaw cut. The three pieces of several children's names are spread on a table and a small group of children put their own name puzzle together.

Name activities demonstrate to children that print is meaningful, that words are composed of letters, and that letters can be named. These early concepts pave the way for later learning to recognize and name upper- and lowercase alphabet letters.

Shared Writing

Shared writing is another activity that demonstrates to children the usefulness of writing. During shared writing, teacher and children cooperatively compose a message that the teacher writes on a large chart. Shared writing is recommended to teach older students about the composing process and the conventions of punctuation, capitalization, and usage (Routman, 2005). For preschoolers, shared writing demonstrates the various ways we use printed texts and provides opportunities for children to learn concepts about print. Writing produced in these activities can take many forms and serve various purposes (e.g., an enlarged get-well card for the classroom assistant who is home with the flu, a graph that presents information about children's favorite farm animals).

Creating a message in shared writing involves three steps: developing concepts and vocabulary before composing the message, composing and writing the message on the chart, and rereading and having children step up to the chart for instruction on the alphabet and print concepts. Details about these steps come later in the chapter. Creating a message demonstrates a variety of concepts about the composing process, including that writers communicate ideas that can be written, writers think as they compose and write, writers generate ideas for writing by talking, writers change ideas and refine their language, and writers consider sequence.

Types of Shared Writing

Shared writing takes a variety of forms based on two purposes. One kind features functional texts in the school environment. These texts include, for example, composing an invitation for a firefighter to visit the classroom, writing a get-well card, reading and writing yard-sale signs and ads, and writing menus. These shared-writing activities support special events in the classroom as well as children's pretend reading and writing in the home-living center, the second dramatic-play center, and the writing center. The second purpose of shared writing relates to ongoing classroom activities and recording information about those events. The content may come from center activities, read-alouds, or conversations about things children have observed. The texts produced during these shared-writing experiences are based on children's experiences and activities within the classroom. This use of "personalized content" provides a familiar context that aids children's comprehension and allows them to focus on learning new strategies for writing.

Functional Texts in the Environment

Shared writing is effective in introducing new forms of functional printed texts that children will encounter as new resources are added to the second themed dramatic-play center or writing center. For example, the home-living center is an ideal place for children to hold a pretend yard sale. Functional texts that relate to yard sales include newspaper ads, yard-sale ads, and yard-sale signs. These texts could be created in shared-writing activities. Newspaper yard-sale ads could be used for read-aloud to help children identify the kinds of information that would be included in their own yard-sale ad or sign. Brainstorming together the messages in these texts that are usually found in

Research Supports Shared Writing

- Through many shared-writing experiences, children gradually acquire an awareness of written words, and the ability to track words from left to right (Morris et al., 2003), a critical precursor of conventional reading.

- Children learn that speech can be written and that print is read from left to right and top to bottom across lines of text. In addition, they learn that words are composed of letters and are separated by spaces (Parkes, 2000).

- Shared writing can be used to help children recognize and write alphabet letters and later to realize that letters in written words are related to sounds in spoken words. They learn to stretch out the sounds in words in order to anticipate which letter their teacher will use to spell the beginnings of some words (Payne & Schulman, 1998).

the home, but not in school, allows children to draw upon their untapped home-literacy knowledge (Duke & Purcell-Gates, 2003). Other functional texts that children may have encountered at home include grocery or to-do lists, gift tags, coupons, baseball trading cards, toy catalogs or brochures, greeting cards, cookbooks, want ads in newspapers, and calendars. Figure 4.8 presents a list of more than 30 different kinds of functional printed texts found in children's environments. These examples provide a wide range of writing forms and purposes that can be used for shared writing.

The functional text developed in shared writing can be placed in the home center or writing center, where children can use it and other printed texts (e.g., birthday cards, parking signs) as models for their own pretend writing. Children are usually eager to write their own messages similar to those that have been created in shared writing. Placing specially prepared materials in at least one center, either the writing center or one of the play centers, provides children opportunities to extend shared-writing experiences.

Recording Information Using Graphic Organizers

Recording information about ongoing classroom activities is another way to engage children in shared writing. These shared-writing experiences could include making a graph to communicate the results of an experiment in which children taste different kinds of toothpaste flavors or one in which they mix colors. Another chart could be made up of facts children learned by observing and exploring a bird's nest and several nonfiction books about birds. Comparing characters found in two different versions of *Goldilocks and the Three Bears* is yet another example. The texts produced during these shared-writing experiences include graphic organizers such as lists, graphs, timelines, Venn diagrams, labeled drawings, and prediction charts. Figure 4.9 (pages 106 and 107) presents examples of nine different kinds of graphic organizers that can be constructed during shared writing.

Shared-Writing Procedures

Regardless of the type of text produced, shared writing includes three major steps: developing concepts and vocabulary before composing the message, composing and writing the message on a chart, and rereading and stepping up to the chart for instruction on the alphabet and print concepts.

Developing Concepts and Vocabulary

The first step in shared writing focuses on showing examples of functional texts, building concepts, and developing vocabulary. There are many kinds of functional texts that are appropriate for preschoolers to create in shared writing (see Figure 4.8 for suggestions). For example, before creating a birthday card, you could read several cards to the children and guide them in making observations about special features that distinguish a birthday card from other kinds of greeting cards.

Functional Printed Texts Found in Children's Environments

- Address books
- Advertisements (newspaper, magazine)
- Applications
- Appointment books and cards
- Bible passages
- Bills
- Brochures
- Calendars
- Catalogs
- Checks
- Cookbooks
- Coupons
- Covers (books, DVDs, records, VCRs)
- Directions
- Forms (order forms, prescription forms)
- Gift tags
- Greeting Cards (Birthday, Get Well, Holiday, Congratulations)
- Instructions
- Invitations
- Labels
- Lists (grocery, to-do, etc.)
- Lottery (and other) tickets
- Magazines
- Maps
- Menus
- Messages
- Money
- Newspapers
- Packages
- Price Tags
- Programs
- Receipts
- Schedules
- Signs (*Do Not Enter*, *Open*, *For Sale*, etc.)
- Sports Trading Cards
- Telephone books

Figure 4.8

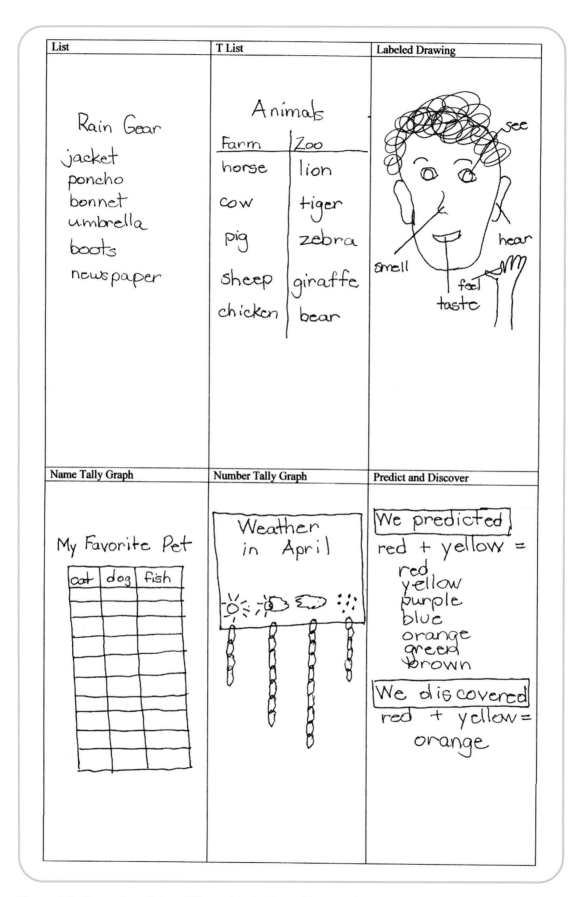

Figure 4.9 *Examples of nine different kinds of graphic organizers constructed during shared writing*

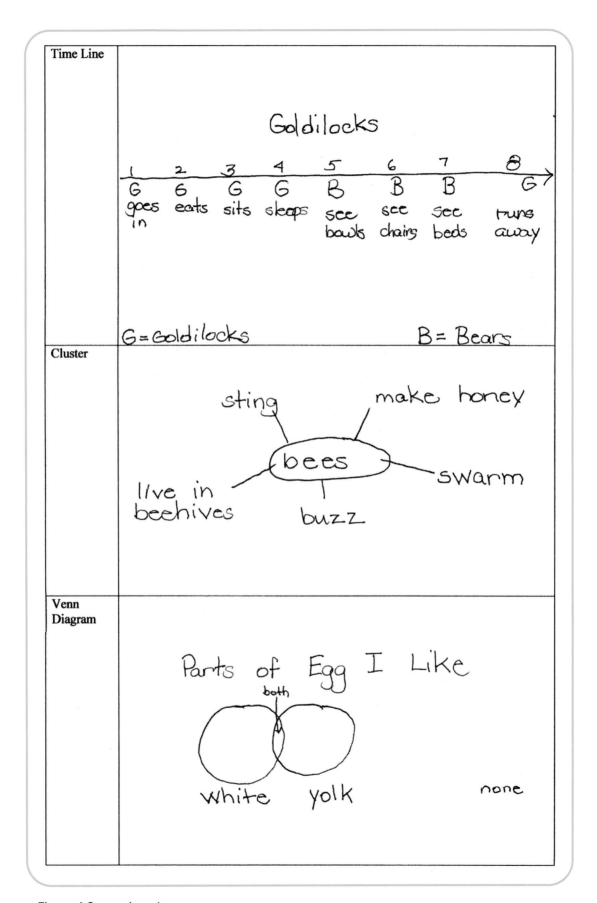

Time Line	Goldilocks
Cluster	bees
Venn Diagram	Parts of Egg I Like

Figure 4.9 *continued*

Shared Writing in Action

Ede Wortham has prepared a shared-writing chart with the title "Things We Will See at the DISL" (Dauphin Island Sea Lab). The children will be going there on a field trip in three days. Ede looks through the book *My Visit to the Aquarium* (Aliki, 1993) with the children and talks about the fish, crabs, lobsters, and sea plants that they will see at the Sea Lab. The children chime in and make comments and ask questions. They note that octopuses sting and sharks bite. Ede assures the children many times that they will not be stung or bitten and that glass walls keep all the animals and people safe. There is a lively discussion about all the sea animals they might see. Because of their enthusiasm about the topic, several children impulsively get up to touch the book as they make comments. Ede skillfully helps them sit back so all can see, then she shows the book more closely to individual children. Ede manages to weave together several threads, drawing children into conversation, managing excited behavior, and delivering information about sea animals.

Then the children read the title of the shared writing twice and offer names of things they will see. Ede asks the children to listen for the beginning and ending sounds of words as she writes and to identify letters she will use to spell the words. Finally, she allows some children to step up to the chart to circle long and short words.

Similarly, concepts and vocabulary are developed prior to shared writing, in which the purpose is to record information using a graphic organizer. In general, three kinds of experiences can be used to build concepts and vocabulary that will be utilized to compose graphic organizers. One experience that builds concepts and vocabulary prior to constructing graphic organizers is to read either a nonfiction informational book or a story aloud. Another method is to engage children in an experience, such as trying out three flavors of toothpaste and deciding which one is their favorite. A third way to build ideas for writing graphic organizers is to bring in objects for children to observe, explore, and discuss. Displaying the title of the text during these prewriting activities can help center children's attention on the topic as well as provide a connection to the next step, writing the shared chart. These experiences provide opportunities for children to encounter new vocabulary, hear the words repeatedly, and use their words in talking about the activity.

Types of Hats

Developing Concepts and Vocabulary

Kay Armstrong brought in to class a collection of hats and talked about when she might wear each hat and what it was made of. She introduced the words *baseball cap, motorcycle helmet, straw hat, rain bonnet, beret, visor,* and *fancy hat* as she shared her hat collection. The children discovered that baseball caps are made of cloth, and straw hats are made of woven straw. A rain bonnet is made of plastic so that it repels water. Kay and the children spent nearly 15 minutes discussing these seven hats. At the end of the discussion, each child was invited to name his or her favorite.

Writing the Shared Chart

The next step in shared writing is composing the chart or message. In this stage of the activity, children observe writing taking place on a large chart that is visible to the group. Typically, the texts are very short so that they can be quickly composed and written. Short texts allow children to remember more of what they have written, which is critical for helping them reread the message, the last stage in shared writing. Of course, as the year progresses, shared writing texts will become longer and more complex, but at the beginning, they may consist of lists of only a few words or phrases.

Types of Hats

Writing the Shared Chart

Kay Armstrong used the experience with the hats to compose two different shared-writing texts on different days. The first day she merely wanted children to remember the different types of hats because she had prepared an art activity of decorating collage hats in the art center. Thus, the title of her first text was "Types of Hats."

She initiated writing the chart by saying, "Today we are going to write a list of types of hats. It says 'Types of Hats' right here [pointing to chart]. Let me read that, 'Types [pointing] of [pointing] Hats' [pointing]. I am first going to write the type of hat you wear to Sunday School. What kind of hat is that, everyone?" Most children responded "fancy hat," and Kay replied, "Yes, I'm going to write 'fancy hat.'" As you can see, Kay selected the text for the shared chart, but all the children had a chance to participate by guessing which word would be written.

Later in the week, Kay created a form that would tally the children's favorite hats as part of a small-group math activity. After showing three of the hats again and having children talk about them, she told the children the tally form would be hanging in the writing center. Sometime during center time, each child was asked to write his or her name on a sticky note and put it on the graph. At the end of the day, Kay and the children counted the number of children whose favorite hat was a baseball hat, helmet, or visor and then discussed which hat more children liked and which hat fewer children liked. The tally form had become a graph that visually displayed the number of children who liked or disliked each of the three hats.

Drawing children's attention to a variety of print concepts is another important feature of shared writing. The following statements and actions provide examples of how to focus children's attention on what happens during writing:

- "Put your eyes up here. I am going to start writing right up here."

- "I'm going to write our first word here." [pointing to the top left side of the chart]

- Demonstrate the left-to-right progression of letters in words.

- "I just wrote the word *fancy*. Now I have to write the word *hat*. I'll scoot my marker over a little to make a space before I start writing that word."

- Pause before writing a word, say the word slowly, and say, "Ffffancy. What sound do you hear at the beginning of that word?" After children isolate the /f/ phoneme, ask, "What letter should I write for that sound?"

As children participate in literacy activities, they have to become familiar with the language we use to talk about these activities. In shared writing, children not only have to think about and attend to the ideas, they also have to develop understanding of the vocabulary we use to refer to what takes place during writing. There are some language patterns that can be used repeatedly in shared writing as well as other activities, such as phonemic awareness and invented spelling (see Chapter 6). Some examples: "What sound do you hear at the beginning of [word]?" "What letter should I write for that sound?" "After I write a word, I leave a space before I start writing the next word." Using the same language to signal activities such as listening to sounds makes tasks more manageable for children.

Rereading and Stepping Up

Written messages are usually intended to be read. For this reason, the last step in shared writing consists of rereading and stepping up, activities that provide children additional literacy experiences centered in topics of immediate and personal interest to them. The procedures for reading the shared chart are similar to those described for shared reading in Chapter 3. These steps provide a structure for rereading and stepping up that is easy for children to follow:

- After writing the entire list, children reread the list two to three times with teacher support.

- Watching the teacher point to each word, the children reread the list from memory.

- Individual children "step up" to the chart and either write on it or point out a particular concept (for example, a letter that appears in their name, the longest word on the chart).

The step-up section of the lesson is used to teach alphabet recognition, letter formation, and concepts about print. There are many tasks that children can complete in step-up: circle a letter they know, circle two letters that are alike, circle a particular letter, point to the space between words, or point to words they want to use in their own writing. Three-year-olds enjoy coming up to the chart and finding an interesting letter. They point to the letter and identify it. (Teachers help children name the letter when needed.) They can also count the number of letters in a word selected by the teacher. Four-year-olds like to step up and select a letter they want to write. They point to the letter, identify it, and then just write it somewhere on the chart. They also enjoy finding long words and counting letters or finding the shortest word. They can find words with four letters, or words that begin with the letter *f*, or words that begin with a capital letter. Figure 4.10 presents a list of possible step-up activities to use in shared writing.

While shared writing can be completed in either whole- or small-group activities, step-up activities are most effective in a small group when all the children in the group can be invited to step up to the chart. When used with the whole class, two or three children step up to the chart. The chart can be placed in a center where the other children are invited to step up to the chart on their own during center time. Having the chart accessible in a center enables you to visit the center during center time and invite children over to step up and show you something interesting on the chart. Most children enjoy these few minutes with you and are eager to step up and count letters, find long and short words, and write on the chart.

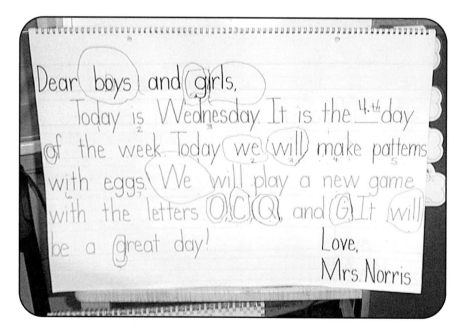

A shared-writing chart in which children have stepped up to circle letters and words

Figure 4.10 Step-Up Activities

Children step up to the shared-writing chart and

- Point to or circle a letter they know
- Point to or circle a letter identified by the teacher
- Point to or circle two letters that are the same
- Point to a letter and write it somewhere on the chart
- Find all the e's (o's, m's, r's, etc.); write that letter on the chart
- Count the letters in a word identified by the teacher
- Find a short word and count the letters
- Find a long word and count the letters
- Find the longest word
- Find a word that begins with a letter identified by the teacher
- Find a word and copy it on the chart
- Point to the first letter in a word
- Circle all the first letters in words in green
- Point to the last letter in a word
- Circle all the last letters in words in red
- Find two words that begin with the same first letter
- Count the number of words
- Circle a word that has the first letter in the child's name

Small-Group Instruction to Guide Writing Practice

Teachers can use small-group time to help children practice writing. Shared writing allows children to see demonstrations of writing and to step up to the chart and write a letter or point to long or short words. Guided practice activities allow children to write for themselves.

Guided Drawing

One way to begin helping children to practice writing is to acknowledge the phase of writing development of the lowest-performing children. I have observed that most 3-year-olds and many 4-year-olds from at-risk homes have few drawing and writing experiences. Therefore, most will be in the scribble phase of writing development. These children will benefit from guided drawing activities that help them make lines, circles, and dots and turn them into symbolic drawings. One guided drawing activity involves making balloons. You demonstrate drawing circles of various colors and then adding long lines for ties on the balloons. As you draw, invite children to talk about where they have seen balloons and which color balloons they like and have drawn. To end the drawing you may say, "I'm going to pretend my balloons are flying in the sky at night. Let me put in some stars around the balloons." Then you demonstrate making various colors of dots. Figure 4.11 presents a sample of a 3-year-old's balloon drawing.

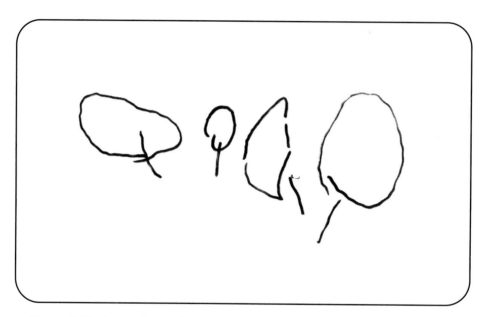

Figure 4.11 *A sample of a 3-year-old's balloon drawing*

Children are not expected to draw perfect lines or shapes or make the drawings clearly representational (look like actual balloons) in this activity. The activity is intended to encourage children's use of language to label circles, dots, lines, colors, and objects drawn. With practice, all children will better control circles, lines (straight, slanted, and curved), and dots. Other activities for guided drawing include having children draw apples (circles with small line stems), lollipops, or chocolate chip cookies (circles with dots inside). A more challenging activity is to make circles and then draw lines connecting all the circles together. Teachers I have worked with call this activity "making a fence." Then children draw a favorite animal inside their fences. Teachers help children draw curved lines by making hills and valleys; they guide children to make slants by drawing slides and skateboard ramps.

Another guided drawing activity is to use lines, dots, and shapes to produce a story drawing (Tompkins, 1980). Figure 4.12 is a drawing produced by a

4-year-old as the teacher guided the drawing and told the story of driving to the library. The drawing has three lines using basic strokes actually found in alphabet letters. To create this drawing, the teacher told the story as she modeled writing each shape she wanted the children to draw. Children drew the shapes and lines as they listened to and watched the teacher.

To draw the picture shown in Figure 4.12, the teacher said, "We are going to drive to the library. The sun is shining. Let's draw the sun. Put a circle, and some lines out. You can make a face on your sun like this [she demonstrates how to draw the sun]. Now we are driving down the road [demonstrates drawing a horizontal line]. We are coming to some mountains. We go up, down, up, down [demonstrates writing slanting lines up and down]. Here is another mountain; let's go up, down, up, down [again demonstrates slanting lines]. We see some trees. Let's draw trees [demonstrates how to draw several vertical lines] and a little hill [demonstrating drawing a hump]." The teacher moved to the next line on the paper and continued her story, "We see a rainbow [demonstrating curved lines] and a fence [demonstrates drawing vertical lines and then a horizontal line through the vertical lines]. Now we see flowers [draws small circles with lines] and a house [draws a square]." The teacher went to the third line of the story and said, "Here are some little flowers [draws several symbols that look like lowercase i]. Oh, oh, the road is curvy here [demonstrates writing an S]. Finally we made it to the library. Let's draw a picture of the book we are going to read [demonstrates how to draw a book]." Notice that the teacher demonstrated making a variety of lines and shapes in sequence from left to right and top to bottom across the paper, each time starting a new line at the left.

Figure 4.12 *A drawing produced by a 4-year-old as the teacher guided the drawing and told the story of driving to the library*

Pretend Writing

Seeing and then practicing familiar, everyday writing routines is another effective small-group technique. Taking telephone messages is one of these routines. Early in the year, one preschool teacher gathers all the telephones in her classroom and home and brings them to class. Each child in the small group has a phone, pencil, and telephone message pad. The teacher demonstrates pretending to answer the phone, hold a conversation, take a phone message for her mother, and write the message. She talks with the children about messages they might take and then all the children around the table answer phones, talk, and write. After three or four minutes when children have taken several messages, the teacher invites one or two children to model for everyone how they take messages. Then the teacher demonstrates how she takes a message when the doctor calls a mother to inquire about a sick baby. Again, the children practice. This teacher also uses small-group time to demonstrate addressing envelopes and writing a grocery list, both using scribbles and copying from empty food containers. For the addresses, children are given the choice of scribble writing or copying their own name and address.

Guided Invented Spelling

Guided invented spelling (McGee & Richgels, 2003) is a systematic approach to helping children spell independently (Bodrova, Leong, Paynter, & Hughes, 2001). This activity is appropriate only for children who know many alphabet letters and recognize many letter-sound relationships. (Chapter 6 describes more direct activities for teaching these concepts.) Guided invented spelling moves children from emergent writing, such as scribbling a menu in the restaurant dramatic-play center, into invented spellings such as spelling *pajamas* "PMZ."

All children first engage in emergent writing, and their writing may include scribbles, mock letters (letter-like forms), symbols, or letters. Emergent writing does not draw upon the alphabetic principle. Children are not attempting to match the words in their message to letters in a systematic fashion. In emergent writing, any letters or scribble can convey the message (see figures 4.1, 4.2, 4.3, and 4.4). On the other hand, invented spelling is when children write messages by carefully matching at least one letter with one phoneme in the words of their messages.

By carefully observing what children do during shared writing, you will know when it is time to begin guided invented spelling for 4-year-olds. Children who are successful at suggesting appropriate beginning letters to spell words during shared writing are ready for guided invented spelling.

Guided invented spelling should occur during small-group work. For her first guided invented-spelling lesson, one preschool teacher prepared a booklet of "Farm Animals," using clip art from the Internet to create a cover page with a barn, and inside pages with illustrations of a pig, cow, and horse, as well as three blank pages. The teacher told the children they would be doing kid writing (Feldgus & Cardonick, 1999) because the kids would be doing the writing. She demonstrated turning to the page with the pig and said, "What will we write on this page? What animal is this?" She told the children that the first step in kid writing was to put down a magic word line. The line is to tell everyone reading the book that this book was written by a kid writer. She told the children to say "pig" slowly, stretching out that first sound. She demonstrated and asked children to suggest a letter to spell that sound. Most of the children suggested P, so she wrote that letter on her magic word line. Because the teacher knew that many children were ready for this new activity, she told the children they were going to listen for the ending sound in *pig*. She demonstrated elongating and isolating the /g/ sound at the end and then asked children to suggest a letter. Children had several ideas including G, Q, and I. As each child suggested a letter, the teacher said, "You are the kid. You decide which letter. I think I'm going to write a *g*. What are you going to write?" She asked each child what they would write and accepted each suggestion.

On the next page of the "Farm Animal" booklet, the children listened to the first and last sound in the word *horse* and most children selected H for the beginning letter and C or S for the ending letter. Spelling *cow* was more difficult. The teacher simply said, "I hear /k/ at the beginning and I could spell that with a K, but I hear /ow/ at the end, and I don't know a letter for that. So I'll just not write a letter." Finally, children were invited to draw a picture and write their own word. Figure 4.13 shows two pages of this kid writing booklet in which the child spelled *pig* "PQ" and drew a farmer, spelled "FR."

Figure 4.13 *Two pages of a writing booklet in which a child spelled* pig *"PQ" and drew a farmer, spelled "FR"*

Routines for Celebrating Writing

When the room is stocked with materials, children observe teachers model reading and writing at the writing center and during shared writing, and after they have guided practice in small groups, most preschoolers find writing irresistible. However, for these young children, the process of pretending to take a telephone message or writing a birthday card is more important than their writing product. I have frequently sat at the writing table with children when birthday cards rapidly become activities for cutting and gluing. It is completely appropriate to allow and encourage children to cut their birthday cards. At the same time, children need to learn that their writing is valued. Therefore, I recommend that you establish a system for saving some examples of writing from all children. This writing can be used in classroom displays and placed in children's portfolio for assessment purposes.

At the beginning of this chapter, you read about how Ede Wortham shared children's writing. Here is another comment from Ede that shows how she values what the children do in writing.

> I am always inspired when I read the writing in the rocking chair. From the scribblers to the "real writers," I believe that acknowledging children's work really does encourage them to write more. The prodding that I do—Are you sure that this is your best work? Tomorrow I want you to add some more details or at least the first sound/letter you hear in the name of your picture—I think is fine because I want them to strive to do a little more each time.

During visits to Ede's classroom, I have noticed that not all children save their writing by placing it in the rocking chair; many children take their writing and place it in their cubby to take home rather than leave it for sharing. Other children simply sweep it up at clean-up time. However, the simple routine that she uses has resulted in a noticeable increase in both the quantity and quality of writing. All of her children are from low-income families, and all have been selected for her preschool program because of low scores on a developmental assessment. Therefore, it is essential that Ede acknowledge their writing as well as model writing daily and allow them the time and space to develop their own control over the content and form of their writing.

Summary

Children seem to go through four distinct phases of writing development, based on how closely their writing resembles conventional alphabet letters and words: scribbling, making letter-like symbols (symbol salad), making conventional letters and recognizing some words, and using invented spelling. All children must develop the "sign concept," the understanding that printed words convey a message. Teachers support children as they pass through these phases in different ways: by guiding children to draw the basic lines and shapes found in all drawing and writing, by helping them to write alphabet letters, and helping them to stretch out the sounds in words. Children's writing in preschool depends on four activities: getting the room reading, providing whole-group demonstrations of writing in use, presenting small-group lessons in which children practice writing, and using daily routines to acknowledge children's writing attempts.

CHAPTER 5

Transforming Direct Instruction in Vocabulary, Alphabet Recognition, and Concepts About Print

Helping children learn the foundational skills and strategies of language and literacy is an important goal in preschool. To ensure that children acquire these understandings, you can plan your program to include instruction that is direct, intentional, and purposeful. Direct instruction includes systematic approaches for which you provide small-group lessons that last 10–20 minutes daily for groups of three to four or eight to nine children, depending on grouping patterns. During small-group instruction, you can guide children's participation and scaffold their responses according to their individual needs. This kind of instruction ensures that you are able to observe children's performance as they engage in a specific task and determine the kind of additional help they may require to be successful.

Direct instruction has not always been a favored method in preschool programs; however, research provides evidence of ways it can be appropriate and effective for young children. Obviously, the most effective preschool program is one that incorporates both direct and embedded instruction in activities that are purposeful and meaningful for children. (For descriptions of research related to direct and embedded instruction, see pages 9–12 in the Introduction.)

Guided Participation

As you work with children to provide them with new knowledge, skills, and strategies, you are attentive to particular strategies for gaining children's attention, helping children sustain attention and participate in the activity. You also respond to individual children's questions, comments, and answers. You can use these strategies during both whole- and small-group activities, but during small-group instruction, you can pay even more particular attention to the individual children with whom you are working. Because there are fewer children to work with in small groups, teachers can craft their instruction to be especially responsive to the needs of individual children, and can help all children gain tools, sometimes called tools of the mind, to help them remember (Bodrova & Leong, 1996).

A Model of Guided Participation in Small-Group Instruction

Because so many children are just developing tools to help them focus and maintain attention, teachers need to use a systematic method to guide children's participation in small-group lessons (Roskos, Tabors, & Lenhart, 2004). Teachers who are skillful in guiding participation know they must be:

- Ready to teach
- Engaging, so that they gain and sustain children's attention
- Focused on the goal of instruction
- Responsive to individual children's responses
- Open and ready to capitalize on opportunities to deepen and expand ideas and to connect to previous and future lessons

(Based on Roskos, Tabors, & Lenhart, 2004).

Key Messages About Direct Instruction

- Direct instruction helps children develop strategies for solving problems, remembering, and paying attention. Children who have not acquired these strategies before attending preschool will benefit from activities that enable them to overcome inattentive, distracted, and impulsive behavior.

- English language learners (ELLs) and other children whose language is underdeveloped need additional instruction to build their vocabularies. Direct instruction provides opportunities that augment what children experience in embedded activities.

- Language scaffolds provide children with models of sophisticated vocabulary and sentence patterns. As teachers use language scaffolds regularly, children become more verbal and gradually begin using the new vocabulary and sentence patterns demonstrated by their teacher.

- Small-group language activities are intended to extend children's use of language for specific purposes (e.g., to describe, to ask questions, to participate in conversations, to plan).

- The number of alphabet letters that children know in preschool and kindergarten is one predictor of children's success in reading and writing in first grade.

- Learning to associate a name with an alphabet letter is a rote memory task.

- In learning the alphabet letters, children must learn about orientation as well other letter features such as straight lines, curved lines, slanted lines, short and long lines, and vertical and horizontal lines. Preschool children never use orientation to distinguish objects.

- Children learn confusable letters (letters which share features) much later than letters that are not confusable.

- Finger-point reading requires children to rely on memory and their concepts about print to match their voices with their eyes and hands. This reading activity is effective for accelerating children's advanced concepts about print. It provides a basis for successful reading and writing in kindergarten.

Being ready to guide participation means that you have all the materials at hand before the lesson is to begin. You know how 3- and 4-year-olds will behave when you don't have the materials prepared beforehand. They will be busy talking and playing, and it may be difficult to gain their attention when you are finally ready to begin. Your preparation should also include a clear understanding of the goals for the lesson and a well-developed mental plan for beginning the lesson, demonstrating activities included in the lesson, and engaging children's participation. You might find it helpful to frame your planning with these questions: *What are we learning? How are we learning? How will we show what we've learned?*

Engaging children can be accomplished in many different ways. You'll want to make eye contact with each child, smile frequently and genuinely, tell children that they are so lucky because today they are going to have fun, lower your voice to a secret whisper, and build anticipation. These opening moves to

Tools of the Mind

A tool helps us do things we could not do by ourselves, such as using scissors to cut cloth. We might be able to tear cloth, but without scissors we could not cut intricate patterns required to make, for example, the front of a jacket. Tools of the mind are strategies that help us use higher mental functions that include focusing our attention on specific items, deliberately remembering information, and thinking logically (Bodrova & Leong, 1996). For example, children who use tools of the mind are able to listen to the teacher without being distracted by noises or movements of other children. They can plan what they will build in the block center and then select particular blocks to build that structure. In other words, tools of the mind are mental strategies that children deliberately use for solving problems, remembering, and attending. Most children are not even aware that they have these strategies because their parents have been helping them learn how to pay attention, remember, and figure out ways to solve problems since they were toddlers. Other children come to school without these tools of the mind, and these children are easy to spot. They are often distracted, act impulsively, and fail to attend to salient features of materials. These children need small-group instruction during which teachers help them gain tools of the mind while teaching them alphabet recognition, vocabulary, and phonemic awareness.

lessons gain children's attention and build excitement. Through voice, facial expression, and body movements, you can capture and hold the attention of wiggling 4-year-olds. You also likely know that keeping little hands occupied is critical. So another engaging move is to plan lessons that get materials into every child's hands. Children are more engaged when they have a set of alphabet letters to sort than if they are merely watching you manipulate alphabet cards.

Because preschoolers' attention can be fleeting, you need to use several strategies to sustain their attention during a lesson that lasts for 10 to 15 minutes. You may find it helpful to plan three different activities to be delivered in that time. Changing activities, but still focusing on the same learning goal, offers several benefits—it keeps children's attention high throughout the lesson and it builds flexible thinking as they apply their new knowledge in different ways. Another way to keep children's attention focused is to intersperse group choral response with individual response. For example, in group choral response, you say, "Everyone find the letter just like mine. It is the letter *T*. Everyone, what letter is this?" In individual response, you say, "Jacoby, find the letter just like mine. What is this letter?" You can cue whether you expect everyone or a particular child to respond before asking questions or giving directions.

When you ask individual children a question, it is important that you remain focused on that child until he or she is successful in answering the question. It does not help the child learn if you invite another child to help out. To help the child respond successfully, you can use scaffolding to reduce the choices.

Capitalizing on children's responses is another way that you can deepen and enrich learning opportunities. For example, the focus of the lesson may be on learning to identify the letters *T*, *L*, and *E*. However, a child may insert the comment, "T is for Tomika." You can quickly pull this additional information into the lesson. "Yes, Tomika's name begins with the letter *T*—/tttttttt/, Tomika. You are so smart." This quick response to the child expands all children's awareness of letters in names and to beginning phonemes. By using children's ideas and connecting them to their experiences, you make lessons richer and more informative.

Using Scaffolding to Guide Participation

You may ask, "Is this a *T* or an *L*?" If the child responds incorrectly, you can provide another scaffold. "This letter has a line across at the top. Could it be a *T*?" If the child still responds incorrectly, you can give the correct answer and have the child repeat it: "This is a *T* because it has a line across the top. Say 'T.'" By using scaffolding in a situation like this, you give the child additional information he or she needs to determine the name of the letter.

Making Decisions About Small-Group Instruction

Typical group arrangements in preschool classrooms include whole group, small group, and very small group. Small groups in preschool are often half the children, with the teacher and teaching assistant splitting the class into two groups of seven to ten children. Very small groups are comprised of no more than three children. These groups usually include children who need more intensive, individualized learning support. The children who most lack tools of the mind (they do not yet know how to maintain attention and seem never to gain concepts) need the personalized instruction provided in very small groups in order to succeed. Because very small group instruction must occur when the other children are at centers, I recommend that you teach only one such group per day. The conversations that you have with children as they play in centers are important for children's language development, and you don't want to lose those opportunities. Consequently, in your planning you will need to consider the balance between interacting with children in centers and using center time to provide very small group instruction.

Vocabulary and Language Expansion

Children's language grows quickly during the preschool years, so that by the time they enter kindergarten, middle-class children know about 5,000 words. After the age of 3, middle-class children learn approximately 2,000 words per year, nearly two words every day (Roskos, Tabors, & Lenhart, 2004). However, children in working-class and poor families know considerably fewer words (Hart & Risely, 1995). And, English language learners (ELLs) may have very little English vocabulary. Because of the critical role of large vocabularies in learning to read and write, you must be deliberate in your planning for all children's language and vocabulary growth. Many of the embedded, child-centered activities I described in chapters 2 and 3—such as repeated interactive read-alouds, shared reading, shared writing, dramatic play, and drama and retelling—will provide language support for children, including ELLs; however, they are not enough for ELLs and children who come to school with underdeveloped language and vocabularies. These children need the experiences that direct instruction provides in frequent small-group language activities. You will also find that scaffolding strategies are helpful during all language interactions.

Language Scaffolding Strategies

Language scaffolds are responses that adults make to children's actions and talk in order to expand their vocabularies and language structures (Roskos,

Tabors, & Lenhart, 2004). These scaffolds are intentional attempts to sustain conversation and provide children with models of new vocabulary and sentence structures. Effective language strategies that you can use are described below (adapted from Roskos, Tabors, & Lenhart, 2004, pp. 40–41):

Elaborating Children's Language

- When answering questions or making comments following children's comments, teachers repeat some of children's words and insert additional information using slightly more complex sentence structure. For example, at breakfast a child holds his milk carton out, expecting the teacher to open it for him. The teacher says, "What would you like me to do?" and the child says, "Open it." The teacher replies, "I would be happy to open your milk carton for you. Watch me. This arrow shows me which side to work on. I pull apart the two sides of the carton. They have been glued together very tightly so I have to peel back a corner to get it started. There, I've peeled apart the two pieces of the carton. Can you pull it all the way?" For ELL children, teachers would greatly simplify their responses, still using some of the children's words and adding more. "I will open your milk. You watch."

Describing Actions

- When teachers are doing an action, they explain what they are doing as they act, using sophisticated vocabulary and specific language. At the writing center, the teacher says, "I am going to write a birthday card today. It is going to be for my sister. Let me get a paper and fold it in half. Now I want to write 'Happy Birthday.'" For ELLs, teachers make sure children are watching and then simply tell what they are doing. "I will fold my paper. Now I will write. I will write 'Happy Birthday.'"

- When children are involved in an activity, teachers explain what children are doing, using sophisticated vocabulary and specific language, and frequently invite children to join the conversation. At the home center the teacher might say, "Marietta, you are getting out some dishes. Will you be making breakfast or lunch?" For ELLs, teachers would describe in more simple language what they are doing: "You got a cup. A cup. Will you drink?"

I Wonder . . .

- When teachers or children are involved in an activity, teachers wonder aloud. At the science center the teacher might say, "I am wondering how to get green. I wonder how I can find out. I think I could mix yellow and blue together. I am wondering what color I will get. I hope it will be green." For ELLs, teacher would deliberately point out objects and pair them with high-utility words, "This is green. This is blue."

Demonstrating and Describing

- Before children are to perform an action, teachers demonstrate the action and describe in detail what they are doing: "We are going to measure flour to make our muffins. We scoop up the flour slowly [demonstrating] and pour it in our measuring cup. It is not full, so we scoop up some more flour [demonstrating] and pour it in our measuring cup again. It is really full now. Now we have to level the flour. Let me show you a trick for leveling the flour. I take this knife and hold it like this against the cup. Then I pull it across the cup very slowly and carefully. Did you see the flour fall down? Good thing I have the cup on this tray to catch the extra flour I pushed off the cup. See, now the flour is level with the top of the cup." For ELLs, the teacher would repeat the most critical vocabulary for actions and objects: "This is flour. We scoop up the flour. We scoop up more flour. We level off the flour."

Sequencing Actions

- Before children are to perform an action, teachers ask children to tell what they will do *first*, *next*, and so on. "Now it is your turn to get a cup of flour and level it off. What do we do first?"

Introducing New Words

- Throughout the day, teachers use both simple everyday words (for ELLs especially) and sophisticated vocabulary to define and explain an object or activity. At the home-living center the teacher might say, "Let's make pancakes. I'm going to turn them over with my pancake turner. This is called a spatula."

These scaffolds wrap language around the child while the child is actively participating in an activity. The language explains and supports the activity even when only the teacher is speaking and children are merely listening. However, as you use language scaffolds throughout each day, you will see that children become more verbal and gradually begin using the new vocabulary and sentence patterns that you have demonstrated.

Vocabulary and Language-Building Activities

There are many language-building activities that occur throughout the preschool day: during transition, center play, outdoor play, and mealtimes. Stepping in and guiding children's pretend play in dramatic-play centers is especially fruitful. Language activities also occur during whole-group activities such as shared reading, repeated interactive read-alouds, shared writing, singing and reciting poems and songs, and dramatizing stories. You will find that these activities can also be used effectively in small groups because they provide each child with more opportunities to participate. In planning small-group language activities, you should be careful to consider the kinds of language you want children to use. Children use language for a variety of purposes: to describe, to convey information, to ask questions to obtain information, to participate in conversations, to express their wants and needs, to plan, to pretend, to answer questions, to recount events from the day or from favorite stories, and to predict.

The best-planned small-group language activities involve you and the children using language for three or more of these purposes. You can plan ahead which vocabulary words will be stressed so that children are exposed to these words multiple times. By planning in this way, you provide a structure for you and children to say words, to classify them into categories, and to use the words in more than one context. The goal for planned vocabulary and language small-group lessons is for children to practice using increasingly complex and varied vocabulary and sentence structures for a variety of different purposes.

Examples of Word Classification Games

- **Packing the Suitcase.** The teacher brings real suitcases packed with clothes. Children help unpack the clothes, and the teachers help them describe the clothes. The teacher passes out photographs of more clothes and, for example, fruit. She tells the children some of the pictures belong in the suitcase because they are clothes, and some of the pictures belong in a fruit bowl because they are fruit. Children either put their picture in the suitcase or a fruit bowl and tell why.

- **Going on a Picnic.** This activity involves unpacking a picnic basket and describing the utensils and plastic food inside. Children can sort pictures of food and animals, for example.

- **Washing Clothes.** Children take clothes out of a laundry basket. They have opportunities to describe the clothes and sort the pieces of clothing from objects that are not clothes. For example, the teacher might introduce toys and ask children to sort toys in a chest and clothes in the clothes basket.

Shared Reading With Planned Language Activities

One kind of planned language activity is to use carefully selected books to scaffold children's attention to verbs, adjectives, and adverbs (Justice, Pense, Beckman, Skibbe, & Wiggins, 2005). Table 5.1 shows how several books can be used to extend children's language. The activities involve retelling, asking and answering questions, pretending, describing, and dramatizing.

Using Category Games to Classify Words

Another small-group language activity involves having children categorize words. Words can be sorted into higher-level categories, including food, furniture, clothes, toys, animals, and pets. Most preschool children can name *apples*, *hamburgers*, and *pizza* but they have difficulty coming up with a name for what we call all of them together: *food*. You can devise games for children that help them learn category names.

Table 5.1 Using Shared Reading to Extend Children's Language

Book	Language Feature	Instructional Activities
Mr. Gumpy's Outing (Burningham, 1970) **Other titles:** *One Dark Night* (Hutchins, 2001) *Do Like a Duck Does!* (Hindley, 2002) *Don't Wake Up the Bear!* (Murray, 2003)	Interesting verbs Animals *flap*, *trample*, *muck*, and *bleat*	Draw attention to actions during read-aloud: • emphasize the verb • define the verb with simple phrases • Ask children to identify other animals that would perform these actions Emphasize the action for each animal in the story Have children use the verbs in various forms (flap, flapped, flapping) in conversation Extend the lesson to provide practice using the vocabulary for different purposes: • Retell the story • Identify animals they would like to be • Pretend to be that animal in the story • Act out the actions of the verbs • Dramatize the story, taking turns being each of the characters *continued on next page*

continued . . .

Book	Language Feature	Instructional Activities
The Napping House (Wood, 1984) **Other titles:** *Who Said Moo?* (Ziefert, 2002) *I Stink!* (McMullan, 2003)	Complex sentences with adjectives Adjective-noun phrases used repeatedly: *cozy bed, snoring, Granny, dreaming child*	Ask questions such as • *Who is snoring?* • *Who else can snore?* • *What is cozy?* • *What else could be cozy?* Repeat and have children repeat adjective-noun phrases as they respond to the questions Expand the activity: • Retell the story • Pretend to be some of the characters • Ask Granny's permission to sleep on the bed • Describe the room in the illustrations as the sun rises
Quick as a Cricket (Wood, 1982)	Adjectives within similes *I'm hot as a fox*	Questioning pattern that extends children's use of both adjectives and the complex sentence pattern incorporating the simile • *What else could be hot?* • Children offer *stove, fire, hair dryer,* and *toaster* • Elaborate on children's responses: *A stove is hot. That's a hot stove.* • Use the pattern from the book: *I'm as hot as a stove* Children pretend to touch the hot stove and act out what they would say and do Children describe their stoves at home

Talking About Themed Objects

Having children explore and talk about objects related to a book or theme is another appropriate language activity. For example, after reading aloud *The Little Red Hen (Makes a Pizza)* (Sturges, 1999), you can bring in a variety of baking pans, including a square glass baking dish, a rectangular aluminum baking dish, an aluminum pie pan, a glass pie pan, an aluminum cake pan, a loaf pan for baking bread, a muffin pan, a round pizza pan, and a rectangular cookie sheet. Each child can be given a baking pan and invited to tell something they know about the pan. You can provide additional information using words described above, as well as words such as *slanted* and *straight* (comparing the sides of a pie pan with the cake pan) or *shallow* and *deep* (comparing the loaf pan with the baking dishes and the cookie sheet). You could also bring in bowls, measuring cups, and spoons, and children could pretend to make batter and pour in into their pan. Following this guided dramatic play, you could place the materials in the home-living center for children's independent exploration.

Alphabet Recognition

Teaching children to recognize and identify alphabet letters is a critical foundational skill. Children's reading and writing in first grade can be predicted by the number of alphabet letters they know in preschool and kindergarten (National Institute of Health and Human Development, 2000). However, it is important to consider exactly what is meant by alphabet recognition. It includes a variety of similar abilities. For example, some children have difficulty remembering the name of an alphabet letter, but when asked to point to a B, for example, on an alphabet chart, they can do so. Of course, most children can sing the alphabet song prior to being able to name letters. Being able to write alphabet letters is another component of alphabet recognition. Finally, being able to name lowercase letters and match upper- and lowercase letters is a component of alphabet recognition. One goal of preschool is to begin teaching children these various skills involved in alphabet recognition.

Beginning With Names

Before teaching isolated letters, teachers I work with always begin the preschool year by using children's names in instruction. Children who've had few experiences with print will not grasp the basic concept that printed text conveys messages or that print is comprised of alphabet letters. Because names are so important to children, we use signatures as a way to call attention to letters. You can add a variety of name games to your activities, including having children match their name and picture, selecting their name from other names that begin with the same letter, and matching letters to letters in their name. Having a "Child of the Day" is a common practice in preschool and is something that can be used to build alphabet recognition. All children can be guided to write that child's name (for 4-year-olds) or match letters to that name (for 3-year-olds). Chapter 4 described this name game activity as well as other name-writing games. These activities pave the way for isolated alphabet-learning activities.

Selecting Letters to Teach

It would seem intuitive to begin teaching the alphabet by starting at the beginning and teaching each letter. Teachers have long used the "letter of the week" approach, and some research has shown it to be effective (Roberts & Neal, 2004). However, research has provided some insight into the nature of learning involved in acquiring alphabet letter names that could suggest another approach to instruction. First, it is important to know that learning to associate a name with an alphabet letter shape is a rote memory task (Treiman & Kessler, 2003). The shape of the letter is arbitrary, as is its name. Children simply have to have a clear image of the letter shape in their mind along with the name, and then be able to match up the shape with the name. The way to this kind of learning is called *paired associative learning.* Children must learn to associate a pair: in this case, the shape with the name. In simple paired associative learning, children are shown a small number of items, such as two to six alphabet letters printed on index cards. Each time they are shown a letter, they are told the letter name and asked to repeat it. After showing all the cards, researchers shuffle the cards and children are shown the cards one at a time again. Children are asked to say the letter name and told the name if they cannot remember. Children continue going through the cards one by one until they can say all letter names correctly. Most teachers add playfulness and other kinds of practice to this basic paired-associative-learning task. By presenting only one pair (in, for example, "letter of the week" instruction), teachers hope children will be more likely to learn that letter name and shape.

However, the second factor in learning to associate a letter shape with a name is that children have to be able to create a distinct visual image of the letter shape. To do this, they must begin to distinguish among the 26 different letter shapes. Therefore, one way to increase the effectiveness of letter learning is to increase children's ability to distinguish between letter shapes, thereby increasing the speed with which children will memorize pairs of shapes and names. Teaching a letter a week does not help children with the problem of being able to distinguish among letter shapes, especially to distinguish between a set of letters that are very similar. Children need to be learning a small set of two to four alphabet letters per week in order to begin the process of distinguishing among the variety of letter shapes.

Learning to distinguish between alphabet letter shapes is difficult for preschoolers because several sets of alphabet letters are very similar to one another. Letters that are hard to distinguish are called "confusable letters" because children so frequently confuse these shapes. Confusable letters include C and U, M, and W, and Z and N. All of these letters have similar features but differ in orientation. Take a plastic letter M, turn it upside down, and it becomes a W. Give a plastic C or Z one-quarter turn and it becomes a U or an N. Preschool children never use orientation to distinguish objects—a book is still a book whether it is held upright or flat (Schickedanz, 1998). Therefore, children must learn about orientation as well as other letter features such as straight lines, curved lines, and slanted lines, short and long lines, and vertical and horizontal lines. Other

Figure 5.1 The Order in Which We Taught the Alphabet Letters Across 19 Weeks of Instruction

UPPERCASE LETTERS

C	O	T
L	E	C
O	F	H
T	I	D
E	H	P
B	S	R
M	A	J
N	K	V
W	X	U
Y	Z	

LOWERCASE LETTERS

c	o	l	
a	d	t	
o	g	e	
l	h	b	
r	n	m	
l	j	p	
v	w	x	
y	k	f	
q	s	u	z

confusable letters include *p*, *b*, *d*, *q*, and *g*; *l*, *i*, and the number *1*; *n*, *h*, and *r*; *w*, *m*, x, *k*, and *y*; and *t* and *f*.

Researchers have shown that children learn confusable letters (letters that share features) much later than letters that are not confusable (Treiman, Tincoff, Rodriguez, Mouzaki, & Francis, 1998). Therefore, the first set of alphabet letters that teachers would teach would include letters that are the most different from one another, such as *C*, *O*, and *T*. Nonetheless, in order to learn all the alphabet letter names, children eventually must get past the obstacle of confusable letter features. Thus, teachers I work with select a set of two, three, or four alphabet letters to work with during a week. After the first few weeks of instruction, one pair of the letters that is taught contains confusable letters with similar features and the other letter or letters are quite distinctive from this pair. We usually teach uppercase letters first and begin with letters that have straight lines and simple circles or curves because we show children how to write letters (for 4-year-olds) as we teach them to distinguish among letter shapes. For example, we may begin with the letters *C*, *O*, and *T* one week and the next week work with *L*, *E*, and *C*. After teaching all the straight and simple curve letters, we teach letters with more complex straights and curves, such as *B*, *S*, and *R*. We teach letters with slants last. Figure 5.1 presents our list of upper- and lowercase letters in the order we teach them.

Introductory Lessons

To introduce children to alphabet letters and guide their awareness of orientation, I have developed letter cards that are long and thin with the letters printed at the top of the cards. The shape of the cards and the placement of the letters allow you to demonstrate orientation so that the letters are at the top of the card. When square shapes are used, young children often turn letters sideways or upside down. Figure 5.2 presents a set of these cards. I use the computer to generate three different fonts of the same letter. In the set presented in Figure 5.2, two letters are introduced each with three different fonts. All children have a set of the six letters and the teacher has a larger set that is more visible to children. Given that children will have different experiences with letters, you may adjust the number of letters and fonts they use in these lessons. With 3-year-olds you may want to only use two kinds of fonts and with 4-year-olds you may introduce three letters instead of two letters. The goals of introductory lessons are to provide ample opportunities for children to:

- Repeat the names of the letter frequently with the teacher's guidance
- Match each of the letters repeatedly to the teacher's model

Let's look at the materials and procedures for this introductory lesson.

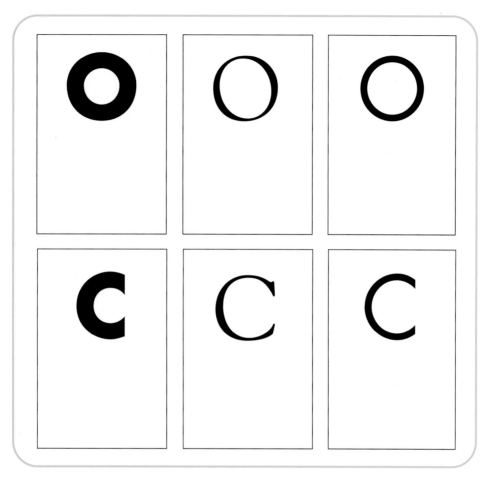

Figure 5.2 *Cards to use in alphabet instruction*

Materials

- Sets of letter cards as shown in Figure 5.2 for each child; use different colors of paper for each set
- Envelopes to hold the sets of letter cards
- Mats made from pieces of construction paper in different colors

Procedures

- Begin by passing out to each child a mat and an envelope containing the letter cards.
- Demonstrate how to spread out the letter cards so they can see all the letters.
- Children spread their letter cards on their mats to keep them organized and not mixed up with other children's cards.
- Hold up a letter and name it.
- Invite children to say the letter name and find one that looks like it.
- Children say the letter name as a group.

- Call on a few individual children to say the letter name.
- Repeat the activity with each letter in each font. (Children do not have to match fonts, merely match letters.)
- For 4-year-olds, end the lesson by having children write each of the letters. Say, "Eyes on me, let me demonstrate." Children write the letter and use "letter formation talk."

Letter formation talk provides directions for children's movement as they write. Figure 5.3 on pages 138 and 139 includes letter formation talk for the upper- and lowercase letters. This is not formal handwriting instruction, which is inappropriate in preschool, where children are expected to write letters correctly on lined paper (Schickedanz & Casbergue, 2004). Here you are merely demonstrating writing letters stroke by stroke on large sheets of unlined paper, and children are not directed to make letters correctly. They are encouraged to write the lines, and you can praise approximations rather than correct formations.

Practice and Assessment Lessons

In the days following the introductory lesson, you can plan three or four practice lessons, using the same set of letters in one or more activities. Each practice lesson ends with having children write letters (for 4-year-olds). Here are several activities you can use to provide children with additional practice:

- *Sort:* Children sort letters into dishes or on sorting mats (papers with large squares or circles on which to sort).
- *Memory match:* A set of cards with at least four copies of each letter are turned face down in the pocket chart. The backs of the cards have color dots or pictures of familiar animals. Children tell the teacher two colors or animals and the teacher turns over the cards. Children in the group must watch as the cards are revealed to know where they can find matches. Teachers draw children's attention to this strategy by reminding them to "remember that *B* and where it is."
- *Fish:* Letters are written on fish-shaped cards, and children select cards using a magnetic rod and identify the letter.
- *Wiggle worm:* Children select tongue depressors out of a plastic cup that have letters or worms printed on them. Children identify the alphabet letter or all children wiggle when they see the worm (can be altered to be a quacking duck, dancing chicken, flapping crow, etc.).
- *Bingo:* Special cards are prepared with the letters of focus printed several times on each card.
- *Letter Writing:* Children use their fingers to "write" letters in a pan filled with shaving cream.

- *Match and Identify:* Children match and identify letters that go in a pattern (E E F T E E F T E E F T).

Reusing the sort activity in another lesson allows you to monitor children's progress. As each child sorts, you can observe which children have correctly sorted. When they have correctly sorted, you can invite children to name each letter, noting who is accurate, who is sometimes accurate, and who is randomly naming letters. Finally, all children write the letter without guidance.

Concepts About Print

Whole-group activities initiate children's learning about print concepts. In shared reading activities, children observe you holding the book upright and turning its pages from front to back as you read aloud. In shared writing, they observe you writing left to right and leaving spaces between the words. In the step-up part of shared writing, they step up and circle words, find long and short words, count the number of letters in words, and find words that begin with a target first letter. Shared writing and step-up also make effective small-group activities for learning about print, especially with 3-year-olds. When children have grasped earlier concepts about print, such as being able to circle words, count letters in words, and find long and short words, they are ready to learn the more complex concept of directionality. Finger-point reading, in particular, is effective for accelerating children's concepts about print. Let's look briefly at how it works.

Small-Group Finger-Point Reading

As we saw in Chapter 3, finger-point reading is when children recite a memorized or nearly memorized text and point to each word as they recite it. You should not confuse this activity with actual or conventional reading. Instead, when children finger-point read, they are relying on memory and their concepts about print to match their voices with their eyes and hands. At first, children will have only a vague notion of how to coordinate what they are saying with their pointing. They may sweep their finger across the text as they have seen their teacher do without regard for the text they are reciting. Later, children may attempt to point to each word as they say it, but they may use the beat of syllables to guide their pointing rather than words and word spaces. You can support this new reading ability by challenging children to use finger-point reading to locate target words. For example, children can be asked to read a sentence from *Brown Bear, Brown Bear, What Do You See?* (Martin, 1967) to locate the words *bear*, *you*, *see*, and *me*.

Figure 5.3 Letter Formation Talk

C	curve, stop
O	curve
T	down, across
L	down, over
E	down, over, over, over
F	down, over, over
H	down, down, across
I	down, across, across
G	curve, line in
Q	curve, line out
B	down, curve, curve
S	curve back, curve forward
D	down, big curve
P	down, curve
R	down, curve, slant out
M	up, slant down, up, down
A	slant up, slant down, across
J	down and curve it up
N	down, slant down, down
K	down, out, out
V	slant down, slant up
W	slant down, up, slant down, up
X	slant down, slant across
U	down, curve it up high
Z	over, slant down, over
Y	slant down and up, with a line down
c	curve, stop
o	curve
l	down
a	curve, line down
t	down, across

d	curve, line up and down
g	curve, line all the way down and curve up
e	line out, curve
h	line down, hump
b	line down, curve around
r	little line, curve up
n	little line, hump
m	little line, hump, hump
i	little line, dot
j	down, dot
p	down, curve
v	slant down, up
w	slant down, up, down, up
x	slant down, slant across
y	slant down, long slant down
k	line, out, out
f	curve and down, across
q	curve, long down and curve up
s	curve back, curve forward
u	down, curve up, down
z	over, slant down, over

Because finger-point reading requires that children memorize the text, texts used for finger-point reading activities must be easily remembered. They should contain short sentences with a total of only 15 to 20 words and may have repetitive patterns. Repetitive texts allow children to see the same word repeated in several places in the text. Nursery rhymes make excellent texts for finger-point reading:

Hickory,   dickory,   dock.
The   mouse   ran   up   the   clock.
The   clock   struck   two
And   down   he   flew.
Hickory,   dickory,   dock.

This rhyme includes rhyming words, repeated words, and a repeated phrase. These help children memorize the text and provide many teaching opportunities. If the texts include alliteration (words with the same beginning sound), you can have children locate words that begin with the same letter and begin helping them learn letter-sound relationships. They can match words, find repeated words, and find words that begin with target letters ("Who can come up and find the word that begins with the letter M?"). In addition to these letter and word activities, you can guide children to finger-point read. As you read the text, demonstrate pointing to each word and have children chime in. Then, invite one child to attempt finger-point reading while the other children say the rhyme. You can guide children's pointing to coordinate it with the chanting of the rhyme. Gradually, by watching you demonstrate and then attempting on their own to finger-point read these short, predictable, and easily remembered texts, children acquire advanced concepts about words and letters and learn to accurately finger-point read.

The most effective finger-point lessons occur when you print text on sentence strips and place them in a pocket chart. Most Big Books and commercial charts include too much text, use fonts too small for children to see, and have word spaces too small for preschoolers to distinguish. The text you prepare is more suitable because it features very large print, has exaggerated word spaces, and no more than four or five words per line. Using a different color for each line of text helps make the text even more readable. The different colors help orient children when they are matching word cards to words on the strips, a very effective activity to build the concept of word.

Summary

Direct instruction in small groups ensures that you are able to give every child the attention he or she needs to learn language effectively. This kind of instruction complements embedded activities because both are designed to facilitate children's language and literacy development. Preschoolers who have not developed strategies for attending and remembering need experiences that guide them in learning how to participate in acceptable ways. It's important to keep activities lively, varied, and short but clearly focused on the learning goals that you have identified.

During the preschool years, children's vocabulary expands rapidly. Some experts suggest that they ought to be learning two new words daily. Language scaffolding strategies are effective in helping build children's vocabulary. These strategies include (1) repeating and adding onto children's comments, (2) demonstrating and describing what you are doing in the demonstration, (3) describing children's actions, (4) wondering aloud, (5) demonstrating and describing what children will do before they act, (6) asking children to describe what they will do next before they act, and (7) using simple and sophisticated vocabulary side by side. Effective small-group language and vocabulary lessons include activities in which children use language for three or more purposes. These activities include using shared reading of books to focus on verbs, adjectives, and adverbs, using "let's explore" activities, and category games. These activities are beneficial for all children, especially those whose language is under-developed and ELLs.

Children have many experiences in embedded, whole-group lessons to learn about the functions and uses of alphabet letters. In small-group lessons, they learn to distinguish among letter shapes, especially letters that are confusable because they have similar features. They also learn about letter formation in informal writing activities. Entertaining practice activities, such as sorting, memory match, wiggle worm, and fish, help children learn important skills in a non-threatening way.

Children develop many concepts about print during preschool as a part of whole- and small-group activities. Finger-point reading is an activity in which children say a memorized text and point to each word as they say it. Although children need many experiences with print before they have some degree of proficiency with the exercise, practicing finger-point reading paves the way for successful reading and writing in kindergarten.

CHAPTER 6

Transforming Direct Instruction in Phonemic Awareness, Alphabetic Principle, and Invented Spelling

Small-group instructional activities are particularly effective in developing children's acquisition of phonemic awareness and the alphabetic principle, concepts that are basic to later success in reading and writing. Phonemic awareness is the ability to hear, distinguish, and manipulate the smallest individual sounds, called phonemes, that make up spoken words. The alphabetic principle is when children realize that the letters in written words correspond to the letters in spoken words. This paves the way for the beginning of phonics instruction, which is learning letter-sound associations. When children have acquired a beginning level of phonemic awareness, discovered the alphabetic principle, and know a few letter sounds, they are ready to participate in guided writing activities that support them as they invent their own spellings. At this early stage of writing, it is critical to encourage children's own spelling rather than teach conventional spelling. Just as children go through developmental stages in learning to talk, they also go through developmental stages in learning to write. Consequently, they need frequent opportunities to use writing for a variety of purposes.

Recall in Chapter 5 the description of scaffolding and its uses to support children's vocabulary and language. This strategy has additional uses in teaching phonemic awareness. In this situation, two kinds of scaffolding can be used: *structural scaffolding* and *instructional scaffolding*. Structural scaffolding is what you do in preparation for a lesson—defining the lesson goal, identifying materials and activities, and establishing guidelines for children's success in the task. In contrast, instructional scaffolding occurs during the lesson, when you provide various levels of support to enable individual children to perform tasks successfully.

Research related to phonemic awareness and the alphabetic principle provides insights into what 3- and 4-year-olds can learn with the support of scaffolded instruction. Some of these findings are summarized here:

- Children's ability to recognize and write alphabet letters is related to their awareness and skill in recognizing and writing their name.

- Knowing a few letter names facilitates children's learning of letter-sound associations. It appears that, even without direct instruction, children are able to deduce relationships between the sounds in letter names and letter sounds (letters such as B and T).

- Children may use alphabet letter-name knowledge to identify phonemes in spoken words and to attach letters with those phonemes to produce spellings for words.

- In training activities, children learned the most letter sounds when the sound was located at the beginning of the letter name (letters such as D and V) and the fewest letter sounds when the letter sound was not in the letter name at all (letters such as W and Y).

Teaching Phonemic Awareness

What is a phoneme? What is phonemic awareness? What is phonics? What is the difference between phonemic awareness and phonics? What is the alphabetic principle? These terms may come into conversations you have with colleagues or children's parents and caregivers, so it is useful to be able to explain the terms in conversational language. On occasion, you may find yourself responding to a parent whose child has used one of these terms. For example, a colleague of mine tells the story of a 4-year-old who complained to his mother that he couldn't get to sleep. His mother suggested that he think of something really boring and that would help him go to sleep. Without hesitation, the 4-year-old replied, "I know what that is. It's phonemic awareness!" This anecdote tells us a lot about that child's thinking and possibly the experience he was having in preschool. Obviously, you want your children to develop a different outlook about this important skill.

Let's look briefly at definitions of terms related to teaching phonemic awareness and phonics.

- **Phoneme:** The smallest part of spoken language or sound. In print, phonemes are represented by letters within *virgules*, or slashes; for example, the phonemes in the word *bat* would be represented in this way: /b/ /a/ /t/. There are three sounds, and those are represented by three letters. The phonemes, or sounds, in the word *boat* would be represented in this way: /b/ /ō/ /t/. There are three sounds, but in conventional spelling, these are represented by four letters. The letters *oa* represent a single sound.

- **Phonemic awareness:** The ability to hear, identify, and manipulate phonemes in spoken words. Phonemic awareness is being able to say, "The first sound I hear in the word *toy* is /t/." One way to think about phonemic awareness is that no print is involved; in fact, you could perform phonemic awareness in the dark. To be phonemically aware, children need only manipulate the sounds and not relate them to letters.

- **Phonics:** Knowledge of letter-sound relationships. Phonics is being able to say, "The word *toy* begins with the letter *T*." In phonics, print is involved; you must be able to see a letter to connect a sound to it.

- **Phonological awareness:** Refers to a general ability to notice the sounds of language. When children recognize that words rhyme, they are demonstrating phonological awareness.

- **Alphabetic principle:** Refers to the realization that the letters in written words are related to the sounds (phonemes) in spoken words. Children demonstrate this knowledge in invented spelling when they use various letters to represent sounds they hear in spoken words (for example, see Figure 4.13 [page 117] which contains invented spellings for *pig* and *farmer*). Children learn the alphabetic principle in reading and writing words.

Key Ideas About Phonemic Awareness

Phonemes can be tricky. When we say words, the sounds that we consider to be phonemes overlap with one another so that they are usually not fully produced as they are when we say the phonemes in isolation. For example, when we say the word *toy*, the phoneme /t/ is immediately pulled into the phoneme /oy/. If you say /t/ in isolation and then say the word *toy*, you will notice that your mouth is in a slightly different position. Therefore, you are articulating the /t/ phoneme slightly differently in isolation and in the word.

We teach children a standard set of sounds associated with the 40 to 44 phonemes that are used to make up all English words. Some phonemes are used more frequently than others, and it is these that are taught in preschool: /b/, /k/, /d/, /f/, /g/, /h/, /j/, /l/, /m/, /n/, /p/, /r/, /s/, /t/, /w/. After children have acquired awareness of these more frequently used consonant phonemes, they can learn /v/, /y/, and /z/. Surprisingly, the phonemes /sh/ and /ch/ are easy for preschoolers to hear and learn as well. However, I do not recommend including these consonant digraphs in letter-sound instruction. I recommend that preschoolers only learn letter-sound relationships for the letters *B, C, D, F, G, H, J, K, L, M, N, P, R, S, T,* and *W.*

Some phonemes are found in alphabet letter names. For example: The letter name *B* consists of two phonemes (/b/ and /ē/); the phoneme associated with the letter *B* (/b/) is found in the beginning of its letter name. The letter name *L* consists of two phonemes (/e/ and /l/); this letter has its phoneme (/l/) at the end of the letter name. In contrast, some alphabet letter names do not include the phoneme. For example, the letter name *G* consists of two phonemes (/j/ and /ē/), neither of which is the phoneme associated with that letter.

Therefore, knowing the names of most of the alphabet letters is important for later helping children learn to say phonemes in isolation. When children learn letter-sound relationships, teachers can make explicit which letters have their phonemes in their names.

Actions Involved in Phonemic Awareness

Many actions are involved in phonemic awareness, and these actions present various levels of difficulty for preschoolers.

- Repeating phonemes in isolation after the teacher is the easiest phonemic awareness action for preschoolers. We ask children to say /j/. Most children in preschool have never said this funny sound before or paid attention to what their mouth is doing when they speak. Even 3-year-olds can be successful at this, and, in short doses, enjoy making these interesting sounds.

- Segmenting or isolating a beginning sound from a spoken word is more challenging for preschoolers. However, many 4-year-olds can be taught to perform this action. Segmenting the ending sound is even more difficult, but some 4-year-olds can accomplish the action with guided instruction.

- Segmenting each phoneme (complete segmentation) in a spoken word develops after children are able to segment beginning and ending phonemes. For example, in complete segmentation, children must say /k/, /a/, /t/, are the sounds in the word *cat*. This action is difficult even for most 4-year-olds, and few children master this task in preschool.

- Blending sounds is an easier task for 4-year-olds. In this action, children are presented with isolated phonemes and they must blend them back to say the word. For example: The teacher says, /k/, /a/, /t/ and the child says the word *cat*.

- Comparing whether two words have the same beginning phoneme is another action that preschoolers find difficult. This action requires the children to hold two words in their memory, segment two beginning phonemes, remember both phonemes, and then judge whether they are the same or different. There are several reasons why this task is beyond most preschoolers: many children are still learning the concepts of "same" and "different;" others cannot hold so many things in their memory; and still other children cannot orchestrate so many mental problems.

Many experts recommend that children be taught to segment sentences into words, words into syllables, and words into onsets (consonants at the beginning of a word) and rimes (the first vowel in a word and all the letters following the vowel) before being taught to isolate phonemes (Walpole & McKenna, 2004). Many children discover on their own how to do these tasks. However, no research has shown that children must learn these before being able to discover phonemes or even if learning to do so makes learning phonemes easier (McGee, 2005). Therefore, I recommend you start with phonemes. For older 3-year-olds, you can build interest in phonemes by playing sound games where children imitate your actions. These are transition activities that children find enjoyable and need take only a minute or so to play. Four-year-olds can begin learning to isolate, blend, and segment phonemes with appropriate teacher support.

Selecting Phonemes to Teach

Teaching two phonemes at a time is the easiest way to help children make progress in phonemic awareness. These phoneme pairs feature different manners of articulation.

For example, the phoneme /s/ is pronounced with the teeth touching, the mouth open, and air is forced through the teeth without voicing. In contrast, the phoneme /m/ is pronounced with the lips closed and pressed together while producing a voiced sound. These two phonemes are usually the first two we teach to children because they are so easily seen and felt on the mouth, one with the mouth open and the other with the mouth closed. Other phoneme pairs that have very different manners of articulation are /d/ and /f/, /k/ and /p/, /b/ and /j/, /l/ and /t/, /g/ and /r/, and /h/ and /n/. These phonemes teach children the general idea of isolating beginning phonemes. Once children get the concept, they learn many beginning phonemes on their own. What is difficult at the beginning is getting 4-year-olds to grasp the concept of listening to the sounds they hear at the beginning of words. Many 4-year-olds need several months of phonemic awareness games before fully gaining the ability to listen for the first sound and isolate it.

> Manner of articulation is the position of the mouth, teeth, tongue, and voice as a phoneme is pronounced.

Scaffolding Children's Participation and Response

Because preschool children may vary greatly in their attempts at isolating beginning phonemes and other phonemic awareness tasks, I recommend scaffolding as a way to be responsive to their individual needs. Scaffolding is the strategic support that teachers provide to facilitate children's accomplishing a task they could not do on their own (Vygotsky, 1978; Wood, Bruner, & Ross, 1976). It can involve a wide range of activities before and during teaching. Consequently, I recommend that teachers use two kinds of scaffolding to make phonemic awareness instruction more powerful. The first kind of scaffold, *structural scaffolding*, takes place before instruction as lessons are planned. *Instructional scaffolding*, the second kind, takes place during the lesson (Ukrainetz & McGee, in preparation).

Structural Scaffolding: Preparing for Phonemic Awareness Instruction

Scaffolding is anything you do to allow a child to perform a task that he or she could not do on his or her own. When you select which two phonemes are to be taught together, you are using a kind of scaffolding. Your choice of phoneme determines the level of difficulty that children may experience with the task. For example, teaching /s/ and /m/ is an easier task for children than teaching /b/ and /p/. That choice, in turn, influences the decisions you make about how you will conduct the lesson: how you will group the children, which materials you will use, how you will introduce the task, how you will invite children to respond (as a group or individually), and how you will respond to their responses, especially when they are unable to perform the action. These decisions are part of structural scaffolding, the planning that you do before you teach the lesson. Here are some guidelines to assist you with structural scaffolding for phonemic awareness instruction:

- *Grouping.* Small or very small groups are most effective. With a small group, you can easily listen to individual children and provide additional help as needed to support each child's opportunity to learn.

- *Materials and Instructional Activities.* These must be engaging for children. (Remember the story of the 4-year-old who was sure that thinking about phonemic awareness would put him to sleep?) Game-like activities using picture cards for isolating, sorting, and matching phonemes are interesting and motivating for children (Ukrainetz, 2006b). Using picture cards instead of letter cards, you can use the same game formats used to teach alphabet recognition: *sort, memory match, wiggle worm,* and *fish.* (See descriptions on pages 136–137 in Chapter 5.) For example, children can sort pictures of objects by their beginning phonemes; play memory match, in which they must match two different pictures with the same beginning sound; play wiggle worm, in which all children must identify the beginning sound of a picture on the tongue depressor or wiggle when they pull out the worm; and fish for cards and to isolate their beginning sounds. These picture card activities provide children with large amounts of practice for learning beginning phonemes in an entertaining format.

- *Children's Responses.* You can have children respond as a group (choral response) or individually. We have found that choral responding is very effective in phonemic awareness activities because it gives all the children more opportunities to answer, reduces wait-time for each child, and keeps the children more involved. However, it is important that periodically teachers identify individual children to respond (Ukrainetz & McGee, in preparation).

By using structural scaffolding during lesson preparation, you give yourself the benefit of knowing that your lessons are going to be interesting, motivating, and successful for the children.

Instructional Scaffolding: Learning to Isolate Beginning Phonemes

Instructional scaffolding, the second kind of scaffolding we recommend for phonemic awareness instruction, takes place during lessons. It provides successively more information for children to use in answering questions teachers ask (Ukrainetz, 2006a). For example, if you were to ask a fairly typical question like "What is the first sound in *moon*?" and a child were unable to answer successfully, the question itself would provide no guidance. However, by using instructional scaffolding at a moment like this, you give the child additional information he or she needs to determine the beginning phoneme. There are three levels of instructional scaffolding available. Whether you need to engage in only one, two, or all three depends on the child and the situation. Remember that preschoolers not only have to attend carefully to the language so they can identify the sounds, they also have to develop understanding of the vocabulary we use to refer to language. Asking a child to listen for a "beginning sound" is a meaningless exercise unless the child understands the concept we are referring to. For these reasons, three levels of instructional scaffolding differ in the amount of guidance they provide for children. Let's look briefly at each level.

Level One Scaffolds: Minimum Guidance

Some children require little support in identifying the first sound in words. With these children, you can use the first level of scaffolding and merely emphasize the beginning sound as you say the word. *"What is the first sound in* mmoon*?"* By elongating the sound only slightly with an exaggerated mouth movement, you are able to draw attention to your mouth and the sound. For phonemes that are not continuants (sounds that can be stretched out and elongated, such as /m/), you can use a more exaggerated action. For example, *"What is the first sound in /d/ /d/ og?"* Here you pop the sound in your mouth one or two times as you say the word.

Level Two Scaffolds: Moderate Guidance

Level two scaffolds provide several additional kinds of information that help children who were not successful with the first level of scaffolding. Here are three ways you can support children's attempts to identify the beginning phoneme: (1) repeat the first sound, elongating it or bouncing the sound several times in isolation before you say the word: (/mmmmmm/ milk or /d/ /d/ /d/ /d/ dog); (2) tell children to watch your mouth as you say the word; and (3) repeat the question and target word as often as you think necessary to help the particular child.

Level Three Scaffolds: Eliciting a Response by Modeling

Level three scaffolds provide the most support and are effective with children who are still unable to isolate the beginning sound with the help provided in level two scaffolds. When you first begin phonemic awareness lessons, you will likely notice that children have difficulty understanding the tasks. Here is an example of a fairly typical exchange during initial phonemic awareness lessons:

Teacher: What is the first sound in *tail*?

Jonathan: Tail.

Teacher: That's the word. Say the sound. Just /t/. We just need the sound.

Teacher: Jonathan, watch my lips. Can you tell me the first sound in /t/ /t/ *tail*? What is the first sound?

Jonathan: Tail.

Teacher: That's the word. Say /t/. The sound is just /t/.

In this example, the teacher provided some level two scaffolds, but they are not enough for the child to be successful. In the next example, the teacher provides a focus for the task and models the correct response, emphasizing the sound in the word and in isolation.

Teacher: We are going to listen for the first sound in the word *jump*. /j/ /j/ /j/ jump. Let's all make /j/ sound. /j/ /j/ /j/. Now you say it: /j/.

Children: /j/ /j/ /j/.

Teacher: You got it. Let's hear it again: /j/.

Children: /j/ /j/ /j/.

Teacher: LiMarvin, let's hear that sound. /j/ in *jump*. /j/.

LiMarvin: /j/ /j/.

Teacher: Oh, you are getting good at that. Amber, let's hear you say /j/ /j/ in *jump*.

Amber: Jump.

Teacher: You got the whole word. How about the first sound, /j/.

Amber: /j/.

Teacher: You got it, Amber. Now everyone, what is the first sound in /j/ /j/ /j/ *jump*?

Children: /j/ /j/ /j/.

Teacher: /j/ /j/ /j/. Good!

As noted earlier, phonemic awareness activities should be engaging and interesting for the children. However, *you* should also enjoy these lessons. Kay Armstrong shares this observation about teaching phonemic awareness. "I love to teach phonemic awareness. I used to talk only about letters and sounds in their names. Now I talk about sounds all the time like, 'That's *kangaroo*, like /k/ in Katie's name.' I would never have thought children could listen to words segmented into phonemes. But with my support, they can listen and count phonemes even when they cannot separate the words themselves."

Adapting Scaffolds to Meet the Needs of Individual Children

As children become more familiar with phonemic awareness tasks, they need less instructional scaffolding support. These examples show how teachers adapted scaffolds in small-group lessons with 4-year-olds who have had a few weeks of phonemic awareness instruction.

Example 1: Rhyming Words

The teacher identified the rhyming words loon *and* tune *from a story. Although the children had heard the words in the story, the teacher anticipated difficulty with identifying /l/ and /t/ so she provided level two instructional scaffolding.*

Teacher:	Let's listen for the first sound in *loon*. What is the first sound, Desiree? /lllllllll/ *loon*. Watch my mouth. /lllllllll/ *loon*.
Desiree:	/l/.
Teacher:	You got it. That was really good. /llllll/ *loon*. Everyone, watch my mouth. /t/ /t/ /t/ *tune*. Everyone, what is the first sound in /t/ /t/ /t/ *tune*?
Children:	/t/.

Example 2: Identifying Beginning Sound

Several weeks later, the teacher was fairly confident of the children's ability to isolate the beginning sound so she first used no scaffolding and then used a level one scaffold:

Teacher:	What is the first sound in *pig*?
Keveon:	[no response]
Teacher:	What is the first sound in /p/ *pig*?
Keveon:	/p/.
Teacher:	Yeah, the first sound is /p/ in *pig*.

Teaching More Advanced Phonemic Awareness Tasks

Recognizing beginning sounds is a first step in developing children's phonemic awareness, and as they become more proficient with the task, they will need less scaffolding support. Eventually, they will be able to answer questions without any scaffolding. When that occurs, they are ready for more challenging phonemic awareness tasks, such as matching words with the same beginning sounds, isolating the final sound, blending, or segmenting. While preschoolers are not expected to master these more difficult tasks, they can be introduced to them. Here again, instructional scaffolding techniques will help children as they learn these new actions.

Phoneme Judging and Matching

Deciding whether or not two words have the same first sound is more difficult then merely isolating a word's first sound. In phoneme judging and matching activities, children must listen to two or more words and judge whether the words' first sounds match (are the same) or do not match (are different). In the next example, children are playing the memory match game and comparing whether two pictures have the same beginning sound. The teacher uses scaffolds in order to make sure the child is successful.

Teacher:	Remember, we have to find two cards that start with the same sound. So let's see what we can find. Devion, it's your turn. Pick up two cards. Okay now, Devion, show us your two cards. Put them down on the table so we can see them. [points to a card] What's that?
Devion:	Pig.
Teacher:	What's the first sound in *pig*?
Devion:	/p/ /p/.
Teacher:	Okay, and what's this? We have it at breakfast sometimes. It's a pancake. What's the first sound in *pancake*?
Devion:	/p/
Teacher:	Are they the same?
Devion:	[no answer].
Teacher:	Let's check the two beginning sounds. What does this start with? [points to pig]
Devion:	/p/.
Teacher:	And this one? [points to pancake]
Devion:	/p/.
Teacher:	/p/p/ pig. /p/p/ pancake. Watch my mouth. Are they the same?
Devion:	[no answer]
Teacher:	Yeah, that's the same sound. /p/ /p/ /p/ in *pig* and /p//p//p/ in *pancake*. Those two go together. They both start with /p/. [The teacher puts the two cards together and gives them to the child.] They are the same so you get to keep them.

The teacher began by reminding children what they were supposed to do: find two cards that start with the same sound. Devion correctly isolated both beginning phonemes without any scaffolds; however, even with level two scaffolds he couldn't judge whether the two sounds were the same. Therefore, the teacher provided a level three scaffold so Devion could accomplish the judging task.

Blending

Blending involves presenting children with a word that is segmented into its individual phonemes and asking them to say the word. This can be a difficult task for preschoolers. One way to simplify the task is to segment the word into its onset and rime (first consonant /p/ and the vowel and everything following it—*eas*—for the word *peas*). In the next example, a group of children are guessing which piece of plastic food the teacher will pull out of a cloth bag. The bag includes a peach, a pear, peas, corn, an apple, and fries.

Teacher: Okay, ready? I'm going to say a funny word and you have to guess what word it is. It will be some of the fruit and things we put in this bag. Let me reach in and get something. Okay, listen carefully. I am holding /p/ /ē/ /z/. Jamarcus, it is /p/ /ē/ /z/.

Jamarcus: Peas.

Teacher: Okay, you got it. It is peas. JaMilya, are you ready? Here's another one. /f/ /r/ /ī/ /z/.

JaMilya: Um.

Teacher: /f/ /r/ /ī/ /z/. /fr/ /ī/ /z/.

JaMilya: Food.

Teacher: Close. It starts with a /f/ sound. Listen again /fr/ /iz/.

JaMilya: Fries.

Teacher: Right. Fries.

In this example, Jamarcus was able to identify the word *peas* when it was completely segmented into its three phonemes. JaMilya needed more scaffolding to identify the word *fries*. At first, the teacher simplified the task by saying the *fr* blended together rather than segmented, and then the teacher simplified the task even further by dividing the word at its onset (/fr/) and rime (/iz/).

Segmentation

Phoneme segmentation is the most difficult phonemic awareness task for most preschoolers to master. Segmenting a word into all of its phonemes places high demands on memory: a single-syllable word may have up to five phonemes (e.g., the word *stripe* is segmented into /s/ /t/ /r/ /ī/ /p/). Despite the challenge involved in segmenting words, phoneme segmentation is the level of awareness required for reading and writing, and all children must eventually master this level of skill to become readers and writers. Most children do not achieve this until late in kindergarten or even first grade. Nonetheless, with scaffolding, preschoolers can enjoy segmenting games.

In the next example, children are playing fish and deciding if the pictures are long words by counting phonemes. Each child catches a "fish," identifies the picture, and counts the phonemes on his or her fingers as the teacher

Scaffolding in Action

Kay Armstrong regularly conducts small-group literacy lessons with her 4-year-old preschoolers. In this lesson, which lasted only 12 minutes, Kay provided mostly level three scaffolds for segmenting, no scaffolds for identifying beginning sounds, and level two scaffolds for identifying ending sounds. This was an early lesson in segmenting, but children had been identifying beginning sounds for several months and had been listening to ending sounds for several weeks.

Kay lays out a line drawing of a train with four boxcars at each place at the horseshoe table. The children quickly find their assigned seat, and Kay begins the lesson.

Kay: "We are going to listen to words, stretch out the sounds, and count how many sounds we hear. Then we are going to put a marker on the train for each sound we hear. I am going to pass around the bag of markers and I want you to count just four markers."

The children count markers out of the bag quickly, as this is a familiar routine. Kay shows the children a picture of a *toe*. She says, "First we will listen to sounds in the word *toe* with our fists, then count, then put markers on the train. Ready. Hold up your fists. The word is *toe*—/t/ /ō/."

Kay segments the word slowly and holds up a finger for each of the two phonemes. Then she asks, "How many phonemes in /t/ /ō/?" The children chime in, saying, "Two."

Then Kay says, "Now we have to count two markers and put them on the train. I'll say the sounds and for each sound you put on a marker: /t/ [pause] /ō/." She demonstrates putting on one marker at a time as she says the phoneme. As she does, she scans all the children to make sure they are following the directions.

Kay shows the next picture, a *bee*. She demonstrates for children how to segment the word, holding up her fist and raising two fingers as she says each phoneme. She has the children segment the word with her again and count the phonemes. Then she demonstrates segmenting the word as the children put down two markers, one at a time as each phoneme is spoken. For this word, Kay asks another question, "Now we know the beginning sound in the word *bee*. What

continued . . .

is it?" All the children chime in, "/b/." Then she says, "Now don't let me trick you. What is the ending sound of *bee*?" She emphasizes the ending sound, but still none of the children respond. She says, "Listen: /b/ /eeeeeeeee/." After elongating the long-*e* sound, many children chime in with that sound.

Kay continues this routine with the words *key*, *bow*, and *see* and then introduces more difficult words: *bat* and *pig*. She continues demonstrating segmenting, counting, and placing markers, having children repeat the segmentation and identify the beginning and ending sounds. She notices that one child, Christian, seems to be segmenting on his own, so she invites him to lead the children in the word *see*. He says /s/ then pauses and looks at Kay. She provides support and very quietly says /eeeee/, and Christian repeats this sound after her. Then all the children segment, count, and place their markers.

scaffolds the entire process. The teacher leads all children to make fists, raise fingers, and count phonemes as she segments the words. As shown in the following example, the children merely raise their fists and count their fingers while the teacher does all the segmenting:

Teacher: You got *cake*, like a birthday cake. Let's all count *cake*. Let's see how big of a fish. Get ready, show us so we can see it. We're gonna count *cake*: /k/ /ā/ /k/ [extending fingers].

Children: /k/ /ā/ /k/ [in unison with teacher modeling].

Teacher: How many sounds?

Child: Four.

Child: Three.

Teacher: Three.

Child: Yes.

The Alphabetic Principle

The alphabetic principle, the realization that letters in written words are related to sounds in spoken words, is a concept that children must acquire to learn to read and write. It is a concept that many preschoolers discover on their own as a result of repeatedly watching their teacher write words and talk about the letters that make up the words. For example, in shared writing children watch you write words beginning with the letter *B* and observe you segment and hear /b/ before writing words beginning with *B*. As a result of these modeling experiences, many 4-year-olds are able to make this critical insight. The alphabetic principle is acquired only in the actual process of reading or spelling words. It is not learned through isolated instruction in letter-sound relationships.

Teaching Letter-Sound Relationships: The Beginning of Phonics Instruction

Children do benefit from instruction in letter-sound relationships when they are ready for this kind of instruction. After several children have discovered the alphabetic principle, the time is right to introduce letter-sound instruction. When children know many alphabet letters and can isolate beginning phonemes, they learn letter-sound relationships very quickly. At that time, you can begin adding letter-sound components to their phonemic awareness activities. Letter-sound instruction should be combined with phonemic awareness instruction to be most effective (National Institute of Child Health and Human Development, 2000).

Alphabet Books

Alphabet books provide many opportunities for children to practice associating phonemes with letters. The best kind of alphabet books for helping children learn letter-sound relationships include a page for each letter, with only a few familiar objects pictured. Many appropriate alphabet books have simple texts, something like, "B is for ball" or "M is for milk." The format of these books makes it easy for you to make letter-sound relationships obvious as you read to children. By saying, "The letter M tells your mouth to say *mmm* at the beginning, *mmm-milk*" (Murray, Stahl, & Ivey, 1996, p. 311), you are helping children make the connection between the letter and its phoneme.

Letter books are another useful resource for children to use to learn letter-sound relationships. Each letter book has only a few pages with pictures of objects beginning with that letter. Placed in the book center or the manipulatives center, these letter and alphabet books are readily available for the children to use independently.

Expanding Phonemic Awareness Lessons to Include Letter-Sound Work

Children who can identify beginning sounds are ready for direct instruction in letter-sound relationships. By combining letters with phonemic awareness games, you can more directly teach letter-sound relationships. Children can sort pictures of objects into boxes labeled with a letter, or fish for a picture and then identify the letter that spells that word. Because phonics is far more complex than simply learning one phoneme attached to one letter, children need opportunities to observe and practice phonics in other activities. Interactive writing, guided invented spelling, and journal writing are meaningful activities through which children learn and apply letter-sound relationships (Strickland & Schickedanz, 2004).

Shared and Interactive Writing

In shared writing, children observe writing taking place. From these observations, children learn that letters represent sounds, letters are used to spell words, and words are made up of letters written in a particular order. They watch and listen as you slowly say words, emphasize phonemes, and match letters with those phonemes. With 4-year-olds, initial spelling demonstrations introduce children to only a few words and then only their first sounds. As children become more aware of letter-sound relationships, more words are spelled, with both beginning and ending phonemes being used.

Interactive writing is a form of shared writing in which children write portions of the message along with the teacher. This activity helps children understand the purpose of writing, learn how to compose a sentence, and learn about sound-letter relationships. Children have the opportunity to write letters associated with sounds in the words. The guided procedure for interactive writing includes these steps:

- With the children, select a topic, a purpose for writing, and compose a sentence.
- Repeat the sentence slowly to help children keep the exact words in mind.
- Hold up a finger (from left to right) for each word in the sentence as you say it.
- Have children repeat the sentence as you again hold up a finger for each word.
- Say a word and slowly stretch out its sound.
- Invite a child to step up to the chart, share the pen, and write the letters associated with the sounds in the word. Help the child articulate the first sound and write a letter. Depending on the length of the word or the complexity of its spelling, you may decide to write the remainder of the word. Or, children may contribute other letters to the word's spelling.
- Reread the sentence, pointing to the words that have been written, and help children recall which word comes next.

- Stretch the next word and invite another child to share the pen. Continue this process until the sentence is complete.

- Reread the complete sentence. Encourage children to talk about the letters they used to write the words or other observations they have about the writing activity.

Because of the complexity of sharing a pen with several students, reading and rereading the sentence, and taking time to stretch out the words, interactive writing usually only comprises one sentence. To ensure that every child has a chance to participate, this activity is best done with small groups or even very small groups.

Supporting Children's Early Attempts at Invented Spelling

Seeing children make the transition from writing with a randomly selected string of letters to using invented spellings is exciting. Invented spellings are a milestone in every child's literacy development (McGee & Richgels, 2004). Some children achieve this milestone in preschool through their own discoveries and good teaching. Other children, even after several months of demonstrations in shared writing and small-group lessons in phonemic awareness and sound-letter correspondences, still need direct instruction to help them begin inventing spellings. (See Chapter 4 for suggestions about guided invented spelling activities to scaffold children as they make their first attempts at inventing spellings.)

For preschoolers, guided invented spelling may consist of writing single words that you have helped them identify. As in interactive writing activities, you scaffold children's attempts by stretching the sounds and helping them select letters to spell those sounds. This activity stretches children's phonemic awareness. It helps children isolate beginning phonemes, then ending phonemes, and finally middle phonemes. This activity also strengthens children's letter-sound knowledge, especially when you point out that two letters can make the same sound but then select the correct letter for that word. For example, "*Cow* can be spelled with a *K*, but it is actually spelled with a *C*. So *C* can make the /k/ sound just like *K*."

The Critical Role of Invented Spelling

Often teachers question the need to have guided invented spelling lessons in preschool. They argue, "Children will begin inventing spellings on their own without teacher input." More important, sometimes preschool teachers are not sure about telling children it is okay to write a word the way they think it should be spelled. They wonder if children will be harmed by spelling words "incorrectly."

I recently observed a guided invented spelling lesson in which an event occurred that demonstrates very clearly the benefits of helping children invent spellings. The teacher had prepared a little booklet with pictures of objects, including a pig, a mop, a bat, and a jet. To guide the invented spelling activities, the teacher reminded children that they would be spelling with letters they wanted to spell with. The children stretched and segmented all three phonemes in the first word, *pig*. The teacher used level three scaffolds to make sure all children were successful. Then she used no scaffolds and asked, "What is the first sound in *pig*?" Several children eagerly replied /p/, while others said the letter *P*. The teacher replied, "*P* is the letter. I want everyone to say the first sound." All the children said /p/, and everyone replied "P" when the teacher said, "Now I want you to tell me the letter." Next, the teacher said, "What sound do we hear next?" and she stretched out the word very slowly. "What sound is in the middle of the word?" One girl responded, " P-I-G spells pig." The teacher ignored this response and again stretched out the word, this time segmenting the middle sound and saying it in isolation. Now, several children articulated the short-*i* sound. Then the teacher asked, "What letter spells that sound?" Some children responded "E," others "A," and the girl once again stated, "P-I-G spells pig." Now the teacher turned to her and said, "What sound do you hear in the middle of pig?" The girl could not respond, so the teacher segmented the word again and repeated the question. Still the girl could not isolate the middle sound, so the teacher said, "/i/ is the middle sound. You say /i/." The girl repeated the sound. Then the teacher asked, "What letter makes that sound?" The girl paused, looked at her neighbor's spelling and replied "E." The teacher was clearly surprised, but said, "Well, you are the kid, so you write what you think."

While the girl had memorized the spelling of the word *pig*, this knowledge did not help her with the process of learning to segment words, hear phonemes, and match phonemes with letters. Granted that listening to middle phonemes and especially knowing short vowel sounds is way beyond what is expected in preschool, the other children were ready for this challenging task. It is not important that children know the correct spelling of the short-*i* sound in the word *pig*; rather it is important they have a strategy for hearing the middle sound in any word. In this lesson, the teacher was teaching a learning strategy rather than teaching how to spell four words. That is the value of guided invented spelling lessons. It provides children with a tool of the mind that can be used in many different situations to allow very young children to write independently. These lessons embed letter-sound instruction in meaningful writing contexts.

Word Building

Building new words from familiar rhyming words is another activity that embeds letter-sound relationships in a meaningful context. This activity is appropriate for 4-year-olds who know many letter-sound relationships and need practice blending onsets and rimes. Children are presented with a familiar word, such as *cat*, using a written word and picture. They listen as you demonstrate how to break the word into two parts: /k/ [pause] /at/. Then you tell the children there are many words in the /at/ family and present a picture of a bat. Children identify the word and, as needed, you guide them in segmenting the word into /b/ [pause] /at/. Next, tell the children that you can spell *bat* using the word *cat*. Place the letters "AT" on a chart. Point out that you are going to spell *bat* by listening for the beginning sound and writing the letter for that sound beside the letters "AT." Using the same procedure, children can spell other words (*fat*, *hat*, *mat*, *rat*).

There are many word families that children can use to build and read new words. Dozens of new words can be built from these common, frequent word families: -at, -ap, -ick, -in, -ip, -op, -ock, -ug, and -uck. The procedure is uncomplicated: start with a picture and word, isolate the word family, and add consonant letters to build words. When children are familiar with this activity, you can introduce "silly" words, reading nonsense words as part of word families. These activities provide early, appropriate practice in blending.

Summary

Phonemic awareness and understanding the alphabetic principle are concepts that preschool children can acquire through scaffolded instruction. As children advance in their understanding of these concepts, they are developing foundational skills for reading and writing. Scaffolded instruction provides children with the levels of guidance they need to move toward independence in identifying beginning sounds, making letter-sound associations, and inventing spelling.

Phonemic awareness includes many different tasks, some much more difficult than others. Children need to be able to imitate a phoneme in isolation, isolate beginning phonemes, isolate ending phonemes, blend onsets and rimes, and judge whether two words have the same phoneme. They must be able to match two pictures with the same beginning phoneme, blend words isolated into phonemes, segment words into onsets and rimes, and finally segment words into phonemes. Many of these tasks are way beyond what a preschool child is expected to do, and even some first graders find all of these tasks difficult to master. However, with scaffolding, preschoolers can participate in activities that call upon many different tasks and gain much ground in acquiring phonemic awareness. Game-like activities are engaging and help sustain children's interest and motivation.

Content for phonemic awareness includes a selection of phonemes based on the manner of articulation. Phonemes that are articulated in very different manners are most appropriate to include in lessons. These phonemes represent the 15 most frequent consonant sounds in English (see page 145) with the possible addition of /sh/ and /ch/, which many children find easy to identify.

Two types of scaffolding are used in teaching phonemic awareness. Structural scaffolding applies to the teacher's planning for the lessons. Instructional scaffolding, which takes place during the lesson, features three different levels. Level one scaffolding consists of minimal additional information of slightly elongating or popping a sound. Level two scaffolding includes a variety of sources of help, such as exaggerating the phoneme by elongating or popping the sound in isolation and in the word, reminding children to look at the teacher's mouth, and repeating the question. Level three scaffolds provide additional structure and modeling, with the teacher saying the word, saying the sound in isolation, and eliciting children to say the sound.

Children who have discovered on their own that letters in written words correspond with sounds in spoken words have acquired an awareness of the alphabetic principle. Learning letter-sound relationships will be accelerated for these children. Their knowledge is expanded in shared and interactive writing, guided invented spelling, and building new words from familiar rhyming words. Invented spelling plays an important role in children's development as writers. In their initial attempts to spell words, children demonstrate their growing ability to connect what they have learned in phonemic awareness lessons to their knowledge of alphabet letters. As children participate in guided invented spelling activities, they are learning strategies that will enable them to write independently.

Final Thoughts on Transforming Preschool Literacy Programs

As I finish this book and reflect back on the incredible journey that I have taken along with the teachers, assistants, and administrators over the past six years, I am truly struck by how much my thinking has changed about what preschoolers can do and how every teacher can best support them in their learning. In 2002 I believed that I knew a great deal about emergent literacy and how to help children begin the transition into more conventional understandings while respecting their playful, individual explorations of written language. It is true that I had experience with some children who were considered at risk, primarily because of family income and the school they would later attend. For the most part, the families of these children were savvy; they secured free all-day preschool for their children. Therefore, the projects I had worked most closely on before 2002 were in public schools and were voluntary and open to all children in a school zone usually with income restrictions.

After 2002, when my first Early Reading First grant was funded, I began working in preschools in both public and private settings. I also began working with teachers with considerably less education and income. As I worked in these Head Start and day care settings, I encountered more families who were less able, for a variety of reasons, to support their young children. Many preschoolers I was now working with came to preschool with even less awareness of the wider world, with less standard language, with less developed oral language, and less experience carrying on extended conversations with adults and other children. I encountered well-meaning and caring teachers who led children through exercises (such as chanting nursery rhymes, counting, saying the ABC's, or naming every child in the classroom) rather than considering what children might be learning during these exercises. Teachers and children were passing time, enjoying themselves for the most part, and keeping safe. They were not developing new concepts about the world, learning to communicate with others in more sophisticated language, or developing an awareness of the places reading and writing could take them.

I found myself convincing teachers that children, all children, could sit in a group and listen to a story all the way through. All children could play games in small groups in which they would develop new literacy and mathematics skills and vocabulary. All children wanted to learn to hold markers and draw and pretend to write. I had to help each transform his or her classroom a little bit at a time, to convince every teacher that what we would learn together would make a difference in children's lives. It was my belief that all teachers could transform their classrooms for their children if only they could find the pathways to begin the process—and that belief has sustained me these past years. All of the transformations I describe in this book might have begun with the germ of an idea in my head, but they blossomed under the hands of the teachers and assistants, as each of them attempted to reach out to their children.

Ede Wortham wears name tags written by her children.

Just last week I received an e-mail from one of the teachers. She wrote,

"Joseph and I spoke again this year at the Alabama Pre-K Conference. Thanks for all the training and support. We are still doing 90% of what we were taught. Children are really learning a lot and growing—85% of students we had last year are on the A & B Honor roll and in advanced reading groups."

It still amazes me that the teachers think that I taught them what they use now; the truth is they taught me more than I ever taught them. I dedicate this book to each and every preschool teacher who has taught me what I needed to know.

Appendix

Monthly Goals for 3-Year-Olds

August and September

Handles books and examines environmental print

- Shows understanding that books are handled in particular ways (awareness of front, back, top, bottom, page turns)
- Shows awareness that print conveys a message by attending to familiar environmental print

Listens to books read aloud and participates in conversations

- Listens with increasing ability to attend to and understand conversations, books, and songs [always a monthly goal]

Plays name games and attends to alphabet letters

- Selects name from a group of other names
- Knows that letters of the alphabet are a special category of visual graphics that can be individually named [differentiates letters from numbers or pictures]
- Sings the ABC song

Participates in nursery rhyme activities

- Recites nursery rhymes with support

Participates in vocabulary games

- Builds understanding of category words (colors, shapes, food, toys, family, friends)

Participates in guided writing and drawing activities

- Attempts to write letter features in guided drawing

October and November

Handles books and examines environmental print

- Shows understanding that books are handled in particular ways (awareness of front, back, top, bottom, page turns)
- Shows awareness that print conveys a message by attending to familiar environmental print

Participates in drama activities

- Begins to dramatize stories with support

Listens to books read aloud and participates in conversations

- Listens with increasing ability to attend to and understand conversations, books, and songs [always a monthly goal]
- Understands, learns, and uses more sophisticated sentences and new vocabulary in conversations and from listening to books in English [always a monthly goal]
- Listens to books in a variety of genres including fiction, nonfiction, and poetry [always a monthly goal]
- Communicates and responds to information, ideas, experiences, feelings, opinions, needs, and questions in conversations with adults and peers [always a monthly goal]

Participates in guided writing and drawing activities

- Uses uncontrolled scribble or one unrefined unit to write name
- Uses linear scribble to write name
- Attempts to write letter features in guided drawing
- Attempts to recognize other children's names

Participates in alphabet learning activities

- Sings the ABC song and attempts to match letters
- Associates a few alphabet letters with people (R is for Ms. Rodgers)
- Recognizes 1–5 alphabet letters
- Recognizes first letter in name

Participates in nursery rhyme activities

- Recites nursery rhymes with support

Participates in vocabulary games

- Builds understanding of category words—(e.g., colors, shapes, home items, food, kitchen supplies, harvest activities [curriculum topic], plant and seeds [curriculum topic]

December and January

Participates in dramatic-play activities, pretending to read and write

- Uses linear scribble to pretend to write in dramatic play

Participates in drama activities

- Dramatizes stories with support

Pretends to read familiar, predictable books

- Memorizes predictable patterns in simple books

Participates in shared reading activities

- Matches letters and words to shared reading charts
- Attempts to count the number of letters in words

Listens to books read aloud and participates in conversations

- Understands, learns, and uses more sophisticated sentences and new vocabulary in conversations and from listening to books in English [always a monthly goal]
- Listens to books in a variety of genres including fiction, nonfiction, and poetry [always a monthly goal]
- Communicates and responds to information, ideas, experiences, feelings, opinions, needs, and questions in conversations with adults and peers [always a monthly goal]
- Follows simple one step directions
- Answers simple *what* and *who* questions about books
- Identifies and interprets objects in illustrations
- Makes comments about book illustrations and events

Practices name writing and participates in guided writing and drawing activities

- Uses uncontrolled scribble or one unrefined unit, to write name
- Uses linear scribble to write name
- Uses some separate units, but not letter approximations, to write name
- Writes mock letters/letter approximations for some letters in name
- Attempts to write letters in guided activities

Engages in alphabet and name recognition games

- Sings the ABC song and matches some letters with singing
- Associates a few alphabet letters with people (*R* is for Ms. Rodgers)
- Recognizes first letter in name, may recognize a few other letters in name

- Recognizes other children's names
- Recognizes 1–5 alphabet letters

Participates in nursery rhyme activities and in language games
- Memorizes and says nursery rhymes with support
- Articulates phonemes with teacher support in playful activities

Participates in vocabulary games
- Builds understanding of more sophisticated category words (e.g., farm and forest animals, clothing, furniture, school items, forest and garden plants)

February and March

Participates in dramatic-play activities, pretending to read and write
- Uses linear scribble to pretend to write in dramatic play

Participates in drama activities
- Dramatizes stories with support

Pretends to read familiar, predictable books
- Matches pretend reading to pages in books
- Memorizes predictable patterns in simple books
- Pretends to read familiar, predictable books with alliteration and rhyme

Participates in shared reading activities
- Matches letters and words to shared reading charts
- Attempts to count the number of letters in words
- Counts letters in words
- Attempts to point to print in shared reading

Listens to books read aloud and participates in conversations
- Understands, learns, and uses more sophisticated sentences and new vocabulary in conversations and from listening to books in English [always a monthly goal]
- Listens with increasing ability to attend to and understand conversations, books, and songs [always a monthly goal]
- Listens to books in a variety of genres including fiction, nonfiction, and poetry [always a monthly goal]
- Communicates and responds to information, ideas, experiences, feelings, opinions, needs, and questions in conversations with adults and peers [always a monthly goal]

- Follows simple two-step directions
- Answers *what* and *who* questions about books
- Identifies and interprets objects in illustrations
- Makes comments about book illustrations and events
- Memorizes predictable patterns in books

Attempts to write name and other letters
- Use some separate units, but not letter approximations, to write name
- Writes mock letters/letter approximations for some letters in name
- Writes name with one or two recognizable letters
- Attempts to write letters

Participates in alphabet learning games
- Sings ABC song and can track most letters
- Recognizes 1–5 alphabet letters
- Recognizes 5–13 alphabet letters
- Recognizes first letter in name and some other letters in name
- Writes 1–5 mock letters or letter approximations

Participates in nursery rhyme activities and in phoneme activities
- Memorizes and says nursery rhymes
- Articulates phonemes with teacher support in playful activities
- Plays rhyming games

Participates in vocabulary games
- Builds understanding of more sophisticated category words
  (e.g., machines, insects, spiders, wind, weather)

April and May

Participates in dramatic-play activities pretending to read and write
- Uses mock letters to pretend to write in dramatic play

Participates in drama activities
- Dramatizes stories

Pretends to read familiar predictable books
- Matches pretend reading to pages in books
- Memorizes predictable patterns in books
- Pretends to read predictable books with alliteration and rhyme

Participates in shared reading activities

- Matches letters and words to shared reading charts
- Counts the number of letters in words
- Attempts to point to words in shared reading
- Counts words in shared reading

Listens to books read aloud and participates in conversations

- Understands, learns, and uses more sophisticated sentences and new vocabulary in conversations and from listening to books in English [always a monthly goal]
- Listens with increasing ability to attend to and understand conversations, books, and songs [always a monthly goal]
- Listens to books in a variety of genres including fiction, nonfiction, and poetry [always a monthly goal]
- Communicates and responds to information, ideas, experiences, feelings, opinions, needs, and questions in conversations with adults and peers [always a monthly goal]
- Follows simple two-step directions
- Answers *what*, *who*, and *why* questions about books
- Identifies and interprets objects in illustrations
- Makes comments about book illustrations and events

Attempts to write name and other letters

- Writes name with one or two recognizable letters
- Writes name with recognizable letters
- Attempts to write letters
- Writes 1—5 mock letters or letter approximations
- Writes 1—5 recognizable letters

Participates in alphabet learning games

- Sings ABC song and can track letters
- Recognizes 1—5 alphabet letters
- Recognizes 5—13 alphabet letters
- Recognizes letters in name

Participates in nursery rhyme activities and in phoneme activities

- Memorizes and says nursery rhymes
- Articulates phonemes with teacher support in playful activities
- Plays rhyming games

Participates in vocabulary games
- Builds understanding of sophisticated category words (e.g., furniture, appliances, shelters, occupations, shopping, restaurants, desert animals and plants, rodeo)

Monthly Goals for 4-Year-Olds

August and September

Participates in environmental print games
- Shows that print conveys meaning by reading familiar environmental print

Handles books and pretends to read
- Pretends to read by attending to illustrations
- Shows understanding that books are read from front to back

Participates in drama
- Dramatizes stories with support

Participates in interactive book read-alouds and conversations
- Understands, learns, and uses more sophisticated sentences and new vocabulary in conversations and from listening to books
- Listens and understands conversations, books, and songs with increasingly complex vocabulary and sentences
- Listens to books in a variety of genres including fantasy, realistic fiction, poetry, and nonfiction
- Communicates and responds to more sophisticated information, ideas, experiences, feelings, opinions, needs, and questions in conversation with adults and peers

Participates in name reading and writing activities
- Identifies own name and names of other children
- Selects name from a group of names
- Identifies names of others from a group of names
- Identifies first letter of own name
- Writes name
- Writes mock letters/letter approximations for all letters in name
- Writes name with a few recognizable letters
- Recognizes 1–5 alphabet letters

Participates in language play activities
- Articulates beginning phonemes (of children's names) with support
- Taps syllables

Participates in nursery rhyme and rhyme book activities
- Memorizes and says nursery rhymes
- Listens to rhyming word books

Participates in vocabulary games
- Develops understanding of simple concept words (e.g., colors, shapes, toys, clothes, food, family, friends)

October and November

Participates in shared writing
- Matches letters and words in shared writing
- Counts words in text

Participates in dramatic-play activities with reading and writing props
- Pretends to write (including during dramatic play)
- Pretends to write for a variety of functional purposes (messages, grocery lists, restaurant orders, and traffic tickets)
- Uses letter strings, mock letters, and symbols to pretend to write
- Dictates stories and other functional texts

Participates in drama
- Dramatizes stories with support

Participates in interactive read-alouds and book conversations
- Understands, learns, and uses more sophisticated sentences and new vocabulary in conversations and from listening to books
- Listens and understands conversations, books, and songs with increasingly complex vocabulary and sentences
- Listens to books in a variety of genres including fantasy, realistic fiction, poetry, and nonfiction
- Communicates and responds to more sophisticated information, ideas, experiences, feelings, opinions, needs, and questions in conversation with adults and peers
- Attempts to answer *who*, *what*, and *why* questions about books (inference and explanation)

Participates in shared reading of predictable books
- Memorizes predictable patterns in books

Participates in name reading and writing activities
- Identifies name and names of other children
- Identifies letters in name
- Identifies beginning letter of several children's names
- Writes name
- Writes mock letters/letter approximations for all letters in name
- Writes name with a few recognizable letters
- Attempts to write all children's names

Participates in alphabet learning games
- Recognizes upper- and lowercase alphabet letters
- Recognizes 1–5 alphabet letters
- Recognizes 5–13 alphabet letters
- Recognizes 13–26 alphabet letters including some lowercase letters
- Writes alphabet letters
- Writes 1–5 recognizable letters (mostly in name)
- Writes 5–13 recognizable alphabet letters including letters not in name

Participates in language play activities
- Taps syllables
- Attempts to sort words by phoneme
- Isolates beginning phonemes with support

Participates in nursery rhyme and rhyme activities
- Memorizes and says nursery rhymes
- Listens to rhyming word books and identifies some rhyming words

Participates in vocabulary games
- Develops concepts about categories (e.g., colors, shapes, kitchen items, home items, harvest activities, plants and seeds, forest animals and plants, farm animals and plants)

December and January

Participates in shared writing
- Uses linear pointing for tracking during shared writing and finger-point reading
- Matches letters and words in shared writing or finger-point texts
- Counts words in text
- Identifies beginning and ending letter of words

- Counts the number of letters in words
- Copies words and writes words with teacher support

Participates in dramatic play with reading and writing props
- Pretends to write for a variety of functional purposes (messages, grocery lists, restaurant orders, and traffic tickets)
- Uses letter strings, mock letters, and symbols to pretend to write
- Dictates stories and other functional texts

Participates in retelling activities
- Retells stories with support
- Retells information books with support

Participates in interactive read-alouds and book conversations
- Understands, learns, and uses more sophisticated sentences and new vocabulary in conversations and from listening to books
- Listens and understands conversations, books, and songs with increasingly complex vocabulary and sentences
- Listens to books in a variety of genres including fantasy, realistic fiction, poetry, and nonfiction
- Communicates and responds to more sophisticated information, ideas, experiences, feelings, opinions, needs, and questions in conversation with adults and peers
- Follows two-step directions
- Answers *who*, *what*, and *why* questions about books (inference and explanation)
- Makes comments about book illustrations that connect to other books
- Connects book information to personal/life experiences

Participates in shared reading of predictable books
- Memorizes predictable patterns in books with advanced syntax

Participates in name activities
- Writes name
- Writes name with nearly all recognizable letters
- Writes name with conventional letters
- Writes other children's names with support

Participates in alphabet learning games
- Recognizes upper- and lowercase alphabet letters

- Recognizes 5–13 alphabet letters
- Recognizes 13–26 alphabet letters including some lowercase letters
- Recognizes 26–40 upper- and lowercase letters
- Writes alphabet letters
- Writes 1–5 recognizable letters (mostly in name)
- Writes 5–13 recognizable alphabet letters including letters not in name

Participates in phonological awareness learning games
- Recognizes rhyming words
- Sorts words by phoneme
- Isolates beginning phonemes in words
- Blends segmented syllables into words
- Learns 1–5 consonant letter-sound associations

Participates in vocabulary games
- Builds understanding of more sophisticated category words (e.g., clothing, furniture, opposites, seasons, winter activities, games)

February and March

Participates in finger-point reading activities
- Uses linear pointing for tracking during finger-point reading
- Uses linear pointing with emphasis on words for tracking during finger-point reading

Pretends to read using memory and linear pointing at words (called "finger-point" reading)
- Matches letters and words in shared-writing or finger-point texts
- Counts words in text
- Locates and identifies words by beginning letter
- Counts the number of letters in words
- Copies words and writes words with teacher support
- Identifies beginning and ending letters of words
- Attempts to match one spoken word or syllable with one written word
- Identifies long and short words

Participates in retelling
- Retells stories with some sophisticated vocabulary with support
- Retells information books with support

Participates in interactive read-alouds and book conversations

- Understands, learns, and uses more sophisticated sentences and new vocabulary in conversations and from listening to books
- Listens and understands conversations, books, and songs with increasingly complex vocabulary and sentences
- Listens to books in a variety of genres including fantasy, realistic fiction, poetry, and nonfiction
- Communicates and responds to more sophisticated information, ideas, experiences, feelings, opinions, needs, and questions in conversation with adults and peers
- Follows two-step directions
- Answers *who*, *what*, and *why* questions about books (inference and explanation)
- Makes comments about book illustrations that connect to other books
- Connects book information to personal/life experiences

Participates in shared book reading of predictable books

- Memorizes predictable patterns in books with advanced syntax

Participates in phonological awareness learning games

- Recognizes rhyming words
- Produces rhyming words
- Recognizes words with the same beginning phoneme with support
- Matches words with same beginning phoneme with support
- Sorts words by phoneme
- Produces a word with the same beginning phoneme
- Isolates beginning phonemes in words
- Blends segmented syllables and onset/rimes into words
- Learns consonant letter-sound associations
- Learns 1–5 consonant letter-sound associations
- Learns 5–10 consonant letter-sound associations
- Attempts to spell words with teacher support
- Attempts to identify new rhyming words in word-building activities

Participates in vocabulary games

- Builds understanding of more sophisticated category words (e.g., machines, insects, spiders, wind, weather, birds)

April and May

Participates in finger-point reading

- Pretends to read using memory and linear pointing at words (called "finger-point" reading)
- Finger-point reads, matching spoken and written words with one to one correspondence
- Attempts to monitor finger-point reading by using beginning-letter sound associations with support
- Attempts to identify words by using memory and tracking
- Locates and identifies words by beginning and ending letter
- Counts the number of letters in words
- Copies words and writes words with teacher support
- Identifies long and short words

Participates in retelling

- Retells stories with some sophisticated vocabulary
- Retells information books

Participates in interactive read-alouds and book conversations

- Understands, learns, and uses more sophisticated sentences and new vocabulary in conversations and from listening to books
- Listens and understands conversations, books, and songs with increasingly complex vocabulary and sentences
- Listens to books in a variety of genres including fantasy, realistic fiction, poetry, and nonfiction
- Communicates and responds to more sophisticated information, ideas, experiences, feelings, opinions, needs, and questions in conversation with adults and peers
- Follows two-step directions
- Answers *who*, *what*, and *why* questions about books (inference and explanation)
- Makes comments about book illustrations that connect to other books
- Connects book information to personal/life experiences

Participates in shared reading of predictable books

- Memorizes predictable patterns in books with advanced syntax

Participates in phonological awareness learning games

- Recognizes rhyming words
- Produces rhyming words
- Reads and spells new rhyming words with teacher support in word-building activities
- Recognizes words with the same beginning phoneme
- Matches words with same beginning phoneme
- Sorts words by phoneme
- Produces a word with the same beginning phoneme
- Isolates beginning and ending phonemes in words
- Blends segmented syllables and onset/rimes into words
- Learns consonant letter-sound associations
- Learns 1–5 consonant letter-sound associations
- Learns 5–10 consonant letter-sound associations
- Learns 10-15 consonant letter-sound associations
- Attempts to spell words with beginning and ending letters with teacher support
- Identifies new rhyming words in word-building activities
- Spells new rhyming words in word-building activities

Participates in vocabulary games

- Builds understanding of more sophisticated category words (e.g., furniture, appliances, shelters, occupations, desert animals and plants, rodeo, cowboys, ranches)

Resources

Children's Literature

Aliki. (1989). *My five senses*. New York: HarperCollins.

Aliki. (1989). *My visit to the aquarium*. New York: HarperTrophy.

Baker, K. (1994). *Big fat hen*. New York: Red Wagon Books.

Barton, B. (1990). *Building a house*. New York: HarperTrophy.

Brown, M. W. (1989). *Big red barn*. New York: HarperCollins.

Burningham, J. (1970). *Mr. Gumpy's outing*. New York: Penguin.

Carlson, N. (1988). *I like me!* New York: Puffin.

Cowley, J. (2003). *Mrs. Wishy-Washy's farm*. New York: Philomel.

Eastman, P. D. (2000). *The alphabet book*. New York: Random House Books for Children.

Galdone, P. (1984). *Henny Penny*. New York: Clarion.

Galdone, P. (1985). *Little red hen*. New York: Clarion.

Gibbons, G. (1988). *Farming*. New York: Holiday House.

Gibbons, G. (1996). *How a house is built*. New York: Holiday House.

Hillenbrand, W. (2002). *Fiddle-I-Fee*. New York: Gulliver Books.

Hindley, J. (2002). *Do like a duck does!* Cambridge, MA: Candlewick Press.

Ho, M. (2000). *Hush!: A Thai lullaby*. New York: Scholastic.

Hutchins, H. (2001). *One dark night*. New York: Viking.

Jones, R. C. (1995). *Matthew and Tilly*. New York: Puffin.

Keats, E. J. (1998). *Peter's chair*. New York: Puffin.

Martin, B., Jr. (1967). *Brown bear, brown bear, what do you see?* New York: Holt, Rinehart, & Winston.

McMullan, K. (2003). *I stink!* New York: Joanna Cottler.

Murry, M. D. (2003). *Don't wake up the bear*. Tarrytown, NY: Marshall Cavendish Children.

Polacco, P. (2003). *G is for goat*. New York: Philomel.

Shannon, D. (1998). *No, David!* New York: The Blue Sky Press.

Sklansky, A.E. (2005). *Where do chicks come from?* New York: HarperCollins.

Stevens, J. (1995). *The three billy goats gruff*. New York: Harcourt.

Sturges, P. (1999). *The little red hen (makes a pizza)*. New York: Dutton Children's Books.

Teague, M. (1994). *Pigsty*. New York: Scholastic.

Tucker, K. (2003). *The seven Chinese sisters*. Morton Grove, IL: Albert Whitman.

Waddell, M. (1991). *Farmer duck*. Cambridge, MA: Candlewick Press.

Waddell, M. (1996). *The pig in a pond*. Cambridge, MA: Candlewick Press.

Walker, C. H. (1992). *Seeds grow*. DeSoto, TX: Wright Group.

Willems, M. (2004). *Knuffle bunny*. New York: Hyperion Books for Children.

Wishinsky, F. (1999). *Oonga boonga: Big brother's magic words*. New York: Corgi Press.

Wood, A. (1982). *Quick as a cricket*. Singapore: Child's Play (International) Ltd.

Wood, A. (1984). *The napping house*. San Diego, CA: Harcourt, Brace, & Company.

Ziefert, H. (1996). *Where is my baby?* Brooklyn, NY: Handprint Books.

Ziefert, H. (2002). *Who said moo?* Brooklyn, NY: Handprint Books.

Professional References

Adams, M., Foorman, B., Lundberg, I., & Beeler, T. (1998). *Phonemic awareness in young children: A classroom curriculum*. Baltimore, MD: Paul H. Brookes.

Barnett, W. S. (2001). Preschool education for economically disadvantaged children: Effects on reading achievement and related outcomes. In S. B. Neuman & D. K. Dickinson (Eds.), *Handbook of early literacy research* (pp. 421–443). New York: Guilford.

Beck, I. L., McKeown, M. G., & Kucan, L. (2002). *Bringing words to life: Robust vocabulary instruction*. New York: Guilford Press.

Benson, P. (1997). Psychological causation and goal-based episodes: Low-income children's emerging narrative skills. *Early Childhood Research Quarterly, 12*, 439–457.

Bloodgood, J. W. (1999). What's in a name? Children's name writing and literacy acquisition. *Reading Research Quarterly, 34*(3), 342–367.

Bodrova, E., & Leong, D. J. (1996). *Tools of the mind: The Vygotskian approach to early childhood education*. Columbus, OH: Merrill.

Bodrova, E., & Leong, D. J. (1998). Scaffolding emergent writing in the zone of proximal development. *Literacy teaching and learning, 3*(2), 1–18.

Bodrova, E., Leong, D. J., Paynter, D. E., & Hughes, C. (2001). *Scaffolding literacy development in the kindergarten classroom*. Aurora, CO: Mid-Continent Research for Education and Learning.

Byrne, B. (1998). *The foundation of literacy: The child's acquisition of the alphabetic principle*. East Sussex, UK: Psychology Press.

Clark, M. (1976). *Young fluent readers*. London: Heinemann Educational Books.

Clay, M. M. (1975). *What did I write?* Portsmouth, NH: Heinemann.

Clay, M. M. (1979). *The early detection of reading difficulties* (2nd ed.). Auckland, New Zealand: Heinemann Educational Books.

Clay, M. M. (1991). *Becoming literate: The construction of inner control.* Auckland, New Zealand: Heinemann Education.

Clay, M. M. (1998). *By different paths to common outcomes.* York, ME: Stenhouse.

Cochran-Smith, M. (1984). *The making of a reader.* Norwood, NJ: Ablex.

Collins, M. F. (2005). ESL preschoolers' English vocabulary acquisition from storybook reading. *Reading Research Quarterly, 40*(4), 406–408.

Cunningham, P. M., & Allington, R.L. (2007). *Classrooms that work: They can all read and write* (4th ed.). Boston, MA: Pearson.

Dickinson, D. K. (2001). Book reading in preschool classrooms: Is recommended practice common? In D. K. Dickinson & P. O. Tabors (Eds.), *Beginning literacy with language: Young children learning at home and school* (pp. 223–255). Baltimore, MD: Paul H. Brookes.

Dickinson, D. K., & Smith, M. W. (1994). Long-term effects of preschool teachers' book readings on low-income children's vocabulary and story comprehension. *Reading Research Quarterly, 29,* 104–122.

Dickinson, D. K., & Sprague, K. E. (2001). The nature and impact of early childhood care environments on the language and early literacy development of children from low-income families. In S.B. Neuman & D.K. Dickinson (Eds.), *Handbook of early literacy research* (pp. 263–280). New York: Guilford.

Dickinson, D. K., & Tabors, P. O. (2001). *Beginning literacy with language.* Baltimore, MD: Paul H. Brookes.

Duckworth, E. (1996). *The having of wonderful ideas and other essays on teaching and learning* (2nd ed.). New York: Teachers College Press.

Duke, N. (2000). Print environments and experiences offered to first-grade students in very low and very high-SES school districts. *Reading Research Quarterly, 35,* 456–457.

Duke, N., & Purcell-Gates, V. (2003). Genres at home and at school: Bridging the known to the new. *The Reading Teacher, 57*(1), 30–37.

Durkin, D. (1966). *Children who read early.* New York: Teachers College Press.

Ehri, L. C., & Sweet, J. (1991). Fingerpoint-reading of memorized text: What enables beginners to process the print? *Reading Research Quarterly, 24,* 442–457.

Fractor, J., Woodruff, M., Martinez, M., & Teale, W. (1993). Let's not miss opportunities to promote voluntary reading: Classroom libraries in elementary school. *The Reading Teacher, 46,* 476–484.

Fraser, B. J. (1991). Two decades of classroom environment research. In B. J. Fraser & H. J. Walberg (Eds.), *Educational environments: Evaluation, antecedents and consequences* (pp. 3–27). New York: Pergamon.

Gardner, H. (1980). *Artful scribbles.* New York: Basic Books.

Halliday, M. A. K. (1975). *Learning how to mean: Explorations in the development of language*. London: Edward Arnold.

Harms, T., Clifford, R., & Cryer, D. (1998). *Early childhood environmental rating scale: Revised Edition*. New York: Teachers College Press.

Harste, J., Burke, C., & Woodward, V. (1983). *The young child as a writer-reader and informant*. Bloomington, IN: Indiana University.

Hart, B., & Risely, T. (1995). *Meaningful differences in the everyday experiences of young American children*. Baltimore, MD: Paul H. Brookes.

International Reading Association and National Association for the Education of Young Children. (1998). *Learning to read and write: Developmentally appropriate practices for young children*. A joint position statement of the International Reading Association (IRA) and the National Association for the Education of Young Children (NAEYC), Adopted 1998. *Young Children, 53*(4), 3–46.

Justice, L. M., & Ezell, H. K. (2002). Use of storybook reading to increase print awareness in at-risk children. *American Journal of Speech-Language Pathology, 11*, 17–29.

Justice, L. M., Chow, S., Capellini, C., Flanigan, K., & Colton, S. (2003). Emergent literacy intervention for vulnerable preschoolers: Relative effects of two approaches. *American Journal of Speech-Language Pathology, 12*, 320–332.

Justice, L. M., Pence, K. L., Beckman, A. R., Skibbe, L.E., & Wiggins, A. K. (2005). *Scaffolding with storybooks: A guide for enhancing young children's language and literacy development*. Newark, DE: The International Reading Association.

Kratcoski, A. M., & Katz, K. B. (1998). Conversing with young language learners in the classroom. *Young Children, 53*, 30–33.

Lomax, R. G., & McGee, L. M. (1987). Young children's concepts about print and reading: Toward a model of word reading acquisition. *Reading Research Quarterly, 22*(2), 237–256.

Martinez, M., Cheney, M., & Teale, W. (1991). Classroom literature activities and kindergartners' dramatic story reenactments. In J. Christie (Ed.), *Play and early literacy development* (pp. 119–140). Albany, NY: State University of New York Press.

Mason, J. (1980). When do children begin to read: An exploration of four year old children's letter and word reading competencies. *Reading Research Quarterly, 15*, 203–227.

McGee, L. M. (2003). Book acting: Storytelling and drama in the early childhood classroom. In. D. Barone & L. Morrow (Eds.) *Research-based practices in early literacy* (pp. 157–172). New York: Guilford.

McGee, L. M., & Morrow, L. M. (2005). *Teaching literacy in kindergarten*. New York: Guilford.

McGee, L. M., & Richgels, D. (2003). *Designing early literacy programs for at-risk preschoolers and kindergartners*. New York: Guilford.

McGee, L. M., & Richgels, D. (2004). *Literacy's beginnings: Supporting young readers and writers* (4th ed.). Boston: Pearson.

McGee, L. M., & Schickedanz, J. (2007). Repeated interactive read alouds in preschool and kindergarten. *The Reading Teacher, 60,* 742–751.

Morris, D., Bloodgood, J. W., Lomax, R. G., & Perney, J. (2003). Developmental steps in learning to read: A longitudinal study in kindergarten and first grade. *Reading Research Quarterly, 38*(3), 302–328.

Morrow, L. M. (1984). Reading stories to young children? Effects of story structure and traditional questioning strategies on comprehension. *Journal of Reading Behavior, 16*(4), 273–288.

Morrow, L. M. (1988). Young children's responses to one-to-one story readings in school settings. *Reading Research Quarterly, 23,* 89–107.

Morrow, L. M., & Rand, M. (1991). Preparing the classroom environment to promote literacy during play. In J. F. Christie (Ed.), *Play and early literacy development* (pp. 141–165). Albany, NY: State University of New York Press.

Morrow, L. M., & Smith, J. K. (1990). The effects of group size on interactive storybook reading. *Reading Research Quarterly, 25,* 213–231.

Murray, B. A., Stahl, S. A., & Ivey, M. G. (1996). Developing phoneme awareness through alphabet books. *Reading and Writing: An Interdisciplinary Journal, 8,* 307–322.

National Institute of Child Health and Human Development. (2000, April). Report of the national reading panel: Teaching children to read. (NIH Publication No. 00-4769). Retrieved February 2, 2005 from http://www.nichd.nig.gov/publications/nrp/smallbook.htm

Neuman, S. B. (1999). Books make a difference: A study of access to literacy. *Reading Research Quarterly, 34,* 286–311.

Neuman, S. B., & Roskos, K. (1992). Literacy objects as cultural tools: Effects on children's literacy behaviors in play. *Reading Research Quarterly, 27,* 202–225.

Neuman, S. B., & Roskos, K. (1993). Access to print for children of poverty: Differential effects of adult mediation and literacy-enriched play settings on environmental and functional print tasks. *American Educational Research Journal, 30,* 95–122.

Neuman, S. B., & Roskos, K. (1997). Literacy knowledge in practice: Context of participation for young writers and readers. *Research Research Quarterly, 32,* 10–32.

Pappas, C. C. (1991). Young children's strategies in learning the "book language" of information books. *Discourse Processes, 14,* 203–225.

Pappas, C. C. (1993). Is narrative "primary"? Some insights from kindergartners' pretend readings of stories and information books. *Journal of Reading Behavior, 25,* 97–129.

Pappas, C. C., & Barry, A. (1997). Scaffolding urban students' initiations: Transactions in reading information books in the read aloud curriculum. In N. J. Karolides (Ed.), *Reader response in elementary classrooms: Quest and discovery* (pp. 215–236). Mahwah, NJ: Erlbaum.

Pappas, C. C., & Brown, E. (1988). The development of children's sense of the written story language register: An analysis of the texture of "pretend reading." *Linguistics in Education, 1,* 45–79.

Paris, A. H., & Paris, S. G. (2003). Assessing narrative comprehension in young children. *Reading Research Quarterly*, 38(1), 36–76.

Parkes, B. (2000). *Read it again!: Revisiting shared reading*. Portland, ME: Stenhouse.

Payne, C., & Schulman, M. (1998). *Getting the most out of morning message and other shared writing lessons*. New York: Scholastic.

Pellegrini, A. D., & Galda, L. (1982). The effects of thematic-fantasy play training on the development of children's story comprehension. *American Educational Research Journal*, 19, 443–452.

Pellegrini, A., & Galda, L. (1990). The joint construction of stories by preschool children and an experimenter. In B. Britton & A. Pellegrini (Eds.), *Narrative thought and written language* (pp. 113–130). Hillsdale, NJ: Lawrence Erlbaum.

Purcell-Gates, V. (1988). Lexical and syntactic knowledge of written narrative held by well-read-to kindergartners and second graders. *Research in the Teaching of English*, 22, 128–160.

Purcell-Gates, V. (1996). Family literacy. In M. Kamil, P. Mosenthal, P. Pearson, & R. Barr (Eds.), *Handbook of reading research* (Vol. 3, pp. 853–870). Mahwah, NJ: Erlbaum.

Purcell-Gates, V. & Dahl, K. (1991). Low-SES children's success and failure at early literacy learning in skills-based classrooms. *Journal of Reading Behavior*, 23, 1–34.

Purcell-Gates, V., Jacobson, E., & Degener, S. (2004). *Print literacy development: Uniting cognitive and social practice theories*. Cambridge, MA: Harvard University Press.

Purcell-Gates, V., McIntyre, E., & Freppon, P. (1995). Learning written storybook language in school: A comparison of low-SES children in a skill-based and whole-language classroom. *American Educational Research Journal*, 30, 659–685.

Richgels, D. J. (2001). Invented spelling, phonemic awareness, and reading and writing instruction. In S. B. Neuman & D. Dickinson (Eds.), *Handbook of early literacy research* (pp. 142–155). New York: Guilford.

Roberts, T. A. (2003). Effects of alphabet-letter instruction on young children's word recognition. *Journal of Educational Psychology*, 95(1), 41–51.

Roberts, R., & Neal, H. (2004). Relationships among preschool English language learners' oral proficiency in English, instructional experience and literacy development. *Contemporary Educational Psychology*, 29(3), 283–311.

Roskos, K., & Neuman, S. B. (2001). Environment and its influences for early literacy teaching and learning. In S. B. Neuman & D. K. Dickinson (Eds.), *Handbook of early literacy research*. (pp. 281–292). New York: Guilford.

Roskos, K. A., Tabors, P. O., & Lenhart, L. A. (2004). *Oral language and early literacy in preschool: Talking, reading, and writing*. Newark, DE: The International Reading Association.

Routman, R. (2005). *Writing essentials: Raising expectations and results while simplifying teaching*. Portsmouth, NH: Heinemann.

Rowe, D. (1998). The literate potentials of book-related dramatic play. *Reading Research Quarterly*, 33, 10–35.

Saltz, E., & Johnson, J. E. (1974). Training for thematic-fantasy play in culturally disadvantaged children: Preliminary results. *Journal of Educational Psychology*.

Schickedanz, J. A. (1998). What is developmentally appropriate practice in early literacy?: Considering the alphabet. In S. B. Neuman & K. A. Roskos (Eds.), *Children achieving: Best practices in early literacy* (pp. 20–37). Newark, DE: The International Reading Association.

Schickedanz, J. A., & Casbergue, R. M. (2004). *Writing in preschool: Learning to orchestrate meaning and marks*. Newark, DE: The International Reading Association.

Schmitt, M. C., Askew, B. J., Fountas, I. C., Lyons, C. A., & Pinnell, G. S. (2005). *Changing futures: The influence of Reading Recovery in the United States*. Worthington, OH: Reading Recovery Council of North America.

Smith, M. W., & Dickinson, D. K. (2002). *User's guide to the early language and literacy classroom observation (ELLCO) toolkit*. Baltimore, MD: Paul H. Brookes.

Smolkin, L. B., & Donovan, C. A. (2002). "Oh, excellent, excellent question!": Developmental differences and comprehension acquisition. In C. Block & M. Pressley (Eds.), *Comprehension instruction: Research-based best practices* (pp. 140–157). New York: Guilford.

Snow, C., Burns, M., & Griffin, P. (Eds.). (1998). *Preventing reading difficulties in young children*. Washington, DC: National Academy Press.

Stein, N., & Glenn, C. (1979). An analysis of story comprehension in elementary school children. In R. Freedle (Ed.), *New directions in discourse processing* (Vol. 2). Norwood, NJ: Ablex.

Strickland, D. S., & Schickedanz, J. A. (2004). *Learning about print in preschool: Working with letters, words, and beginning links with phonemic awareness*. Newark, DE: The International Reading Association.

Taylor, D., & Dorsey-Gains, C. (1988). *Growing up literate: Learning from inner-city families*. Portsmouth, NH: Heinemann.

Taylor, N., Blum, I., & Logsdon, D. (1986). The development of written language awareness: Environmental aspects and program characteristics. *Reading Research Quarterly, 21*, 132–149.

Teale, W. H. (1978). Positive environments for learning to read: What studies of early readers tell us. *Language Arts, 55*, 922–932.

Tompkins, G. E. (1980). Let's go on a bear hunt! A fresh approach to penmanship drill. *Language Arts, 57*, 782–786.

Treiman, R., & Kessler, B. (2003). The role of letter names in the acquisition of literacy. In R.V. Kail (Ed.), *Advances in child development and behavior* (Vol. 31, pp. 105–135). Oxford, UK: Academic Press.

Treiman, R., Tincoff, R., Rodriguez, K., Mouzaki, A., & Francis, D. (1998). The foundations of literacy: Learning the sounds of letters. *Child Development, 69*, 1524–1540.

Ukrainetz, T. A. (2006a). Assessment and intervention within a contextualized skill framework. In T. A. Ukrainetz (Ed.), *Contextualized language intervention: Scaffolding PreK–12 literacy achievement* (pp. 7–58). Eau Claire, WI: Thinking Publications.

Ukrainetz, T. A. (2006b). Scaffolding young children into phonemic awareness. In T. A. Ukrainetz (Ed.), *Contextualized language intervention: Scaffolding preK–12 literacy achievement* (pp. 429–467). Eau Claire, WI: Thinking Publications.

Ukrainetz, T. A., & McGee, L. M. (in preparation). Responsive instruction: Scaffolding young children's phonemic awareness.

Ukrainetz, T. A., Cooney, M. H., Dyer, S. K., Kysar, A. J., & Harris, T. J. (2000). An investigation into teaching phonemic awareness through shared reading and writing. *Early Childhood Research Quarterly, 15,* 331–355.

Van den Broek, P. (1994). Comprehension and memory of narrative texts: Inferences and coherence. In M. A. Gernsbacher (Ed.), *Handbook of Psycholinguistics* (pp. 539–588). San Diego, CA: Academic Press.

Van den Broek, P. (2001). The role of television viewing on the development of reading comprehension. Washington, DC: U.S. Department of Education.

Van Kleek, A., Gillam, R. B., & McFadden, T. U. (1998). A study of classroom-based phonological awareness training for preschoolers with speech and/or language disorders. *American Journal of Speech-Language Pathology, 7,* 65–76.

Vygotsky, L. S. (1978). *Mind in society: The development of higher psychological processes.* Cambridge, MA: Harvard University Press.

Walpole, S., & McKenna, M. C. (2004). *The literacy coach's handbook: A guide to research-based practice.* New York: The Guilford.

Weinstein, C. S. (1979). The physical environment of the school: A review of the research. *Review of Educational Research, 49,* 577–610.

Whitehurst, G. J., Arnold, D. S., Epstein, J.N., & Angell, A. L. (1994). A picture book reading intervention in day care and home for children from low-income families. *Developmental Psychology, 30*(5), 679–689.

Whitehurst, G. J., Crone, D. A., Zevnbergen, A. A., Schultz, M. D., Velting, O. N., & Fischel, J. E. (1999). Outcomes of an emergent literacy intervention from Head Start through second grade. *Journal of Educational Psychology, 91,* 261–272.

Williamson, P. A., & Silvern, S. B. (1991). Thematic-fantasy play and story comprehension. In J. Christie (Ed.), *Play and early literacy development* (pp. 69–90). Albany, NY: State University of New York Press.

Wood, D., Bruner, J., & Ross, G. (1976). The role of tutoring in problem solving. *Journal of Child Psychology and Psychiatry, 17,* 89–100.

Worden, P. E., & Boettcher, W. (1990). Young children's acquisition of alphabet knowledge. *Journal of Reading Behavior, 22*(3), 277–295.

Index